The Illustrator's Guide

to Law and Business Practice

Simon Stern

AOI the Association of Illustrators

Published in the United Kingdom by
The Association of Illustrators
150 Curtain Road London EC2A 3AT

The right of Simon Stern to be identified as the author of the work has been asserted by him in accordance with the Copyright Design and Patents Act 1988.

British Library Cataloguing in Publication Data.

A catalogue record of this book is available from the British Library.

ISBN 978-0-9558076-0-2

Contents

Introduction to the 2008 edition

The original edition of this guide, *Rights,* was published in 1986, the result of 'shadow-reading' my stepdaughter's textbooks on the law of trusts and the law of contract. The law of trusts must be one of the most opaque and terminally boring subjects ever devised, but to my surprise I found contract law to be interesting, understandable and, above all, very relevant to my own everyday practice as an illustrator. Without knowing it I had been making contracts practically every day of my life.

When, armed with the knowledge I had gleaned from G. H. Treitel's *The Law of Contract,* I managed to see off one of IPC's then notorious copyright grabs, out-arguing their in-house lawyer, I decided I ought to pass on what I had discovered to my fellow illustrators. So the original version – *Rights* – was born. In many ways it was very unsatisfactory – incomplete, awkwardly written in parts and, above all, it had no index. 'Never mind,' I thought, 'it's better than nothing and I can revise it in a year or so.' Twenty-one years later I have finally got round to making that revision, and I apologise for the delay.

This new edition has been almost completely re-written, and in the process acquired a new title. I have added a good deal of new material and simplified some unnecessary complications (particularly in the 'Royalties' section). Realizing that many illustrators find this amount of legal stuff hard going, I have divided the guide up into three sections – *Must Read, Should Read* and *Read When Needed.* A rag-bag of subjects which needed to be included but didn't seem to me to merit a section of their own have been included in the appendices. Above all, I have added the much-needed index.

I hope illustrators, their agents, and teachers will find it useful as a guide and source of reference.

Simon Stern 2008

Disclaimer

The good news is that because I am myself an illustrator, this guide is written entirely from an illustrator's point of view. It deals with those situations that arise from time to time in every illustrator's life, and ignores many of the byways of copyright and contract law which are unlikely to be relevant.

The bad news is that I am not a qualified lawyer, and although I have done my best not to mislead in any way, and though Robert Lands, who is a real lawyer, has kindly checked through the guide looking for mistakes in the legal bits, readers must bear this in mind. *Caveat lector.* You have been warned.

Simon Stern

AOI

14 Rules to Keep you out of trouble

1

Man eating crocodiles (particularly partial to creative types)

1 | 14 Rules to keep you out of trouble

Many people find reading about the law quite hard going. This is the most important part of the *must read* section which offers illustrators a few rules to follow to keep themselves out of trouble. It's no substitute for reading other parts of the guide, but it's better than nothing

Yum

1:1 Give yourself time

Commissions usually happen on the phone when you're in the middle of something else, and it's easy to be caught by surprise and end up agreeing to stuff you shouldn't. Don't let yourself be rushed. Ask lots of questions before committing yourself. If necessary, offer to ring the client back in a specified time when you have had time to think about it. Always sound enthusiastic, relaxed, and friendly, but be prepared to say 'no'. What you agree to at this stage will form the basis of a binding contract. (For more negotiating hints, see Section 6). Clients will very often be willing to change their contract terms, and some clients routinely 'try on' rights grab contracts before sending you a decent one. (If you don't know what a rights grab is, then you *really* need this guide. See Appendix A).

1:2 Use the AOI Terms and Conditions

Once you have sorted out the terms for the job, best practice is to use the AOI Terms and Conditions (unless the client has sent you a contract, in which case see below). These make clear to the client the terms on which you propose to undertake the commission, and are especially important with high-value or complex jobs. To be legally binding they should be sent to the client *as soon as the commission is agreed,* and a copy should be kept.

By using them at the first opportunity you give the client a chance to raise any objections, and you ensure that they form part of the contract and can be relied upon if things go wrong later. All agents use terms of trade like these routinely for every job they do, so clients are used to them.

Even if you have not sent them at this early stage, it is still worth sending them later – preferably with the rough, rather than waiting until you send in the artwork. Although they will not form part of the original contract, they will still have considerable value as evidence of what your understanding of the contract is. *However, the only way to be sure that your terms of trade form the contract is to send them at the earliest opportunity, as a written acceptance of the client's offer.*

1:3 Confirm agreements in writing

If you haven't used the AOI Terms and Conditions you can still help yourself by confirming any verbal agreements in writing soon after you have made them, and keeping a copy. Email is probably the best and easiest way of doing this.

1:4 Keep your old briefs, roughs and notes

Not forever, of course, but for a reasonable time. If a dispute arises, they are good documentary evidence and may be important. It's a good idea to jot down (on the brief or separately) any verbal agreement you make as evidence, should you need it, of what has been agreed.

1:5 Always read client's contracts

I know it's tedious, but it's really important to read the client's contract if you are sent one. Some are OK, but often they're not. Client's terms and conditions are drawn up by their lawyers with the client's interests in mind, usually at the expense of the illustrator's.

They sometimes demand ownership of the artwork, and the disadvantages of this are obvious. They sometimes involve complete assignments of copyright, which are hardly ever justified by the circumstances, and attempts by a client to obtain the copyright (rights grabs) should almost always be strongly resisted. (See Appendix A).

If you receive unacceptable terms from the client, speak to the commissioning editor/designer about it if the deadline is looming and you need to get it sorted. Otherwise simply strike out the offending clauses and send it back (keeping a copy), or send your own terms and conditions in their place (see 8:15, *The Battle of the Forms*). Many clients are prepared to alter their standard terms if requested.

In cases where the client's terms need to be signed and returned, some illustrators assume that by not signing they will have avoided agreeing to them. This is not the case. The illustrator's silence, followed by performance of the commission, will imply consent. (see 8:15).

1:6 Get advice if you need it

Get it from anywhere you can. The AOI will advise members on legal questions, contracts and prices for free. They also publish a review of fees, which is updated periodically.

1:7 Use the AOI Ownership of Artwork stickers

Or make a version of your own, and stick it on the front of your artwork or on the cover sheet (not on the back where no one will see it). It is now generally accepted in the industry that the illustrator owns his/her artwork unless otherwise agreed but there are still a few clients who are unaware of it.

The AOI sticker tells all the people who handle the artwork – from art director to printer – that it is yours and must be returned.

Some wonderful clients send back artwork as a matter of course. Do not make a habit of picking up artwork yourself unless time hangs heavy on your hands. Instead, write to the art director and ask for it to be returned by messenger or registered post. Writing is better than phoning, as you will then have a record of your request.

1:8 Don't copy other people's images (and that includes photographs)

If you do, you could be sued by the photographer or artist for infringement of copyright. Flipping an image, or making a painterly version of a photograph is not usually enough to keep you out of trouble[2]. If you take a 'substantial' part of someone else's image and use it in your own, both you and your client could be in trouble. This applies to all copyright works, including paintings, photographs, sculptures and 'works of artistic craftsmanship', unless their creators have been dead for 70 years (in which case they are out of copyright)[3]. You can use the information in a photograph, but you must not copy a substantial part of it.

1:9 Deadlines are sacred

If you agree to a deadline, you must try to keep to it. If the client has any sense, there will be some contingency time, but there may not be. If you need more time, let the client know straight away. Try not to agree to deadlines that you cannot keep. This applies particularly to long jobs (for instance children's books) where it is easy to be over-optimistic and clients can sometimes pile on unreasonable pressure. If you miss a deadline badly the client may be entitled to look to you for compensation for any losses it suffers as a result.

1:10 Always get advice on royalty contracts, and never begin substantive work on a picture book until the contract's agreed

Royalty contracts are long and complex, and publishers expect you to negotiate the details. Some book packagers are particularly inclined to send contracts late in the day, when work is well under way. This is very unprofessional, and the sign of a possibly dodgy publisher. If the contract is unacceptable to the illustrator, but the job is already half done, this can leave both parties in a very difficult position, so don't let it happen. (Section 10 provides a good outline guide to royalty contracts).

1:11 Treat amateur clients with care

Clients who are not used to commissioning illustration are often a problem because they don't understand the normal ground-rules. It is all the more important to make sure that they know the terms of the agreement they are making with the illustrator. It is wise to explain to them verbally such basic things as ownership of artwork, who has the copyright, and rejection fees.

1:12 Beware of agents with contracts

Most illustrators' agents do not have formal contracts, and those UK agents that do often have bad ones.[4] So if offered a formal contract by an agent, read it carefully and get advice. Check if the agent is a member of the Society of Artists' Agents, who have a good code of conduct (see Appendix F) and are generally to be trusted.

1:13 Never cheat on your agent

Illustrators have been known to go behind their agents' backs and accept a job 'on the side' to avoid paying the agent's commission. *Don't even think about it.* Not only is it unethical, but it is a breach of your (informal) contract[5], and the agent will almost certainly find out and never trust you again.

1:14 Never assign copyright (well, hardly ever)

This should go without saying, but in case you are in any doubt, here are the reasons –

Money. The whole economy of illustration works on the basis that clients buy different types of licence, and pay according to the extent of the use they have bought. This breaks down if it becomes normal for clients to acquire copyright, since as the copyright owner the client can use the image for whatever it wants, and even sell it on to third parties, without paying the illustrator a penny more.

Loss of control. It's bad enough to have your image used without restriction by the original client, but once copyright is transferred there is nothing to stop it being sold on to, say, an image bank, who will have to pay nothing for its use of the image. In that case the original illustrator will find himself potentially competing with (and being undercut by) his own work, or may find his image being used in a context which he objects to. The illustrator himself will have no right to reproduce his own image once copyright has been assigned.

Loss of future earnings. If the illustrator retains the copyright, he can on retirement exploit his past work in image banks if he wishes. He is also entitled to payment for secondary uses, such as photocopying, which he cannot claim for if he is not the copyright owner.

Distortions. Rights Grabs (demands for copyright assignment) inevitably include a waiver of moral rights, including the right of integrity. So the illustrator may have his work changed, distorted or used out of context, and will have no redress.

There are a very few cases where a copyright assignment may be appropriate –

Trade marks. By their nature trade marks require almost every sort of use in all media. For this reason copyright is often assigned to the client, and trade mark fees are usually very high.

Films and other projects involving a very large number of different copyrights. It is sometimes customary to assign copyright in such cases, mainly for ease of administration.

Loads of money. If a client really wants copyright *and is prepared to pay for it,* it may be reasonable to assign it. The price of a copyright buyout should be very high.

2. In fact you could end up in greater trouble, as the photographer may claim you have treated his work in a derogatory fashion (see 7:24 'Moral Rights').

3. There are some limited exceptions to this. See 7:5 'Permitted Acts and Fair Dealing'.

4. I have seen some decent agents' contracts from America, especially second rights and merchandising agents, so this is not an invariable rule. If your main market is the USA (eg greetings cards), a USA agent is well worth considering.

5. See 8:4.

AO I

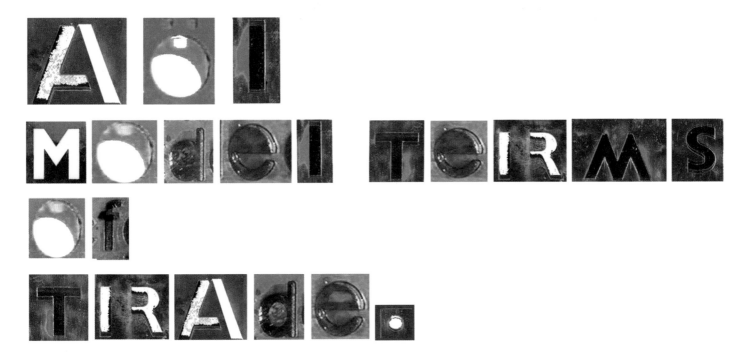

A o I
model terms
of
trade.

2 & 3

2 | The AOI model terms of trade

This set of terms of trade are intended for use by illustrators and their agents. It is suitable for most flat-fee commissions, but not for royalties. Very complex jobs involving several stages may require a special contract.

The AOI model terms of trade can be freely photocopied, scanned or reset (unlike the rest of this book) by anyone who wishes. We suggest you copy them onto an A4 sheet (front and back) and add your name and contact details at the top.

The front of the form requires the illustrator/agent to fill in the relevant details. The back of the form contains the details of the contract, the proverbial 'small print'. There is no need for the client to sign and return this form; it is legally binding unless the client objects to the terms it contains. (Why? See 8:1, 8:5 and 8:15).

The contract has been drafted with the aim of protecting the client's interests as well as the illustrator's, which inevitably involves a certain amount of compromise. The various clauses are explained in detail in the next section.

This contract can be modified if you wish, but we would very strongly advise you not to do so without getting qualified legal advice, not least because contracts which are ambiguous or nonsensical will be interpreted by the courts against the interests of whoever issued the contract.

Illustration by Lyn Moran

Acceptance of Commission

To _____

I am pleased to accept your commission for artwork as follows:

Title/subject _____

Commissioned by _____

Delivery date [roughs] _____ [artwork] _____

Fee £ _____ plus VAT _____ Agreed expenses £ _____ Plus VAT _____

Terms of copyright licence to be granted

Customer's name (end-user) _____

Use _____

Area covered by licence _____

Duration _____

Exclusivity: the licence is exclusive to the end-user unless otherwise stated below.

Credits: a credit for editorial work is required. A credit for non-editorial work is not required unless so stated below.

Special terms (if any) _____

_____

_____

The Standard Terms and Conditions for this commission and for the later licensing of any rights are shown on the back of this page. Please review them together with the above and let me know immediately if you have any objection or queries. Otherwise you will be deemed to have accepted them.

Signature of illustrator _____ Date _____

This commission is subject to all the terms and conditions on the reverse side.

Terms and conditions

Ownership of copyright/Copyright licence

1. The copyright in artwork commissioned by the Client shall be retained by the Illustrator.

2. The Client or the Client's customer (where the Client is acting as an intermediary) is granted a licence to reproduce the artwork solely for the purposes set out on the face of this acceptance of commission. If the acceptance of commission is silent, the Client or the Client's customer is granted an exclusive licence for one time use in the United Kingdom only.

3. During the currency of the licence the Illustrator shall notify the Client of any proposed exploitation of the artwork for purposes other than self-promotion and the Client shall have the right to make reasonable objections if such exploitation is likely to be detrimental to the business of the Client or the Client's customer.

4. Where use of the artwork is restricted, the Illustrator will normally grant the Client or the Client's customer a licence for use for other purposes subject to payment of a further fee in line with current licensing rates to be mutually agreed between the Illustrator and Client.

5. The licence hereby granted to use the artwork is contingent upon the Illustrator having received payment in full of all monies due to her/him and no reproduction or publication rights are granted unless and until all sums due under this Agreement have been paid.

6. The licence hereby granted is personal to the Client or the Client's customer (where the Client is acting as an intermediary) and the rights may not be assigned or sub-licensed to third parties without the Illustrator's consent.

Payment

7. The Client shall pay all invoices within 30 days of their receipt. Interest at a rate of 2% per month is payable on any balance unpaid after 30 days of the date of invoice.

Cancellation

8. If a commission is cancelled by the Client **through no fault of the Illustrator**, the Client shall pay a cancellation fee as follows:

(i) 25% of the agreed fee if the commission is cancelled before delivery of roughs;

(ii) 33% of the agreed fee if the commission is cancelled at the rough stage;

(iii) 100% of the agreed fee if the commission is cancelled on the delivery of artwork;

(iv) pro rata if the commission is cancelled at an intermediate stage.

9. In the event of cancellation, ownership of all rights granted under this Agreement shall revert to the Illustrator unless the artwork is based on the Client's visual or otherwise agreed.

Delivery

10. The Illustrator shall use her/his best endeavours to deliver the artwork to the Client by the agreed date and shall notify the Client of any anticipated delay at the first opportunity in which case the Client may (unless the delay is the fault of the Client) make time of the essence and cancel the commission without payment in the event of the Illustrator failing to meet the agreed date.

11. **The illustrator shall not be liable for any consequential loss or damages arising from late delivery of the artwork.**

12. The Client shall make an immediate objection upon delivery if the artwork is not in accordance with the brief. If such objection is not received by the Illustrator within 21 days of delivery of artwork it shall be conclusively presumed that the artwork is acceptable.

Approval/Rejection

13. Should the artwork fail to satisfy, the Client may reject the artwork upon payment of a rejection fee as follows:

(i) 25% of the agreed fee if the artwork is rejected at the rough stage;

(ii) 50% of the agreed fee if the artwork is rejected on delivery.

14. In the event of rejection, ownership of all rights granted under this Agreement shall revert to the Illustrator unless the artwork is based on the Client's visual or otherwise agreed.

Changes

15. If the Client changes the brief and requires subsequent changes, additions or variations, the Illustrator may require additional payment for such work. The Illustrator may refuse to carry out changes, additions or variations which substantially change the nature of the commission.

16. **No distortion or cropping shall be made to the reproduced image without prior notice to or consultation with the Illustrator.**

Warranties

17. Except where artwork is based on reference material or visuals supplied by the Client or where otherwise agreed, the Illustrator warrants that the artwork is original and does not infringe any existing copyright and further warrants that she/he has not used the artwork elsewhere.

18. The Client warrants that any necessary permissions have been obtained for the agreed use of reference material or visuals supplied by the Client or its customer and shall indemnify the Illustrator against any and all claims and expenses including reasonable legal fees arising from the Illustrator's use of any materials provided by the Client or its customer.

Ownership of artwork

19. The Illustrator shall retain ownership of all artwork (including roughs and other materials) delivered to the Client.

20. The Illustrator's original artwork shall not be intentionally destroyed, damaged, altered, retouched, modified or changed in any way whatsoever without the written consent of the Illustrator.

21. The Client shall return all artwork to the Illustrator not later than 6 months after delivery in undamaged, unaltered and unretouched condition although the Client may make and retain transparencies or scans to enable it to exploit the rights granted with the artwork.

22. If the artwork is lost or damaged at any time whilst in the Client's custody (which shall mean any time between delivery of artwork to the Client and its safe return to the Illustrator) the Client shall pay compensation to the Illustrator for the loss/damage of the artwork at a rate to be agreed or, in default of agreement, decided by the Ethics Committee of the Association of Illustrators.

23. **The client shall not be liable for any consequential loss or damages arising from loss or damage to the artwork.**

Credits/Moral rights

24. The Client shall ensure the Illustrator is credited in any editorial use of the artwork. Credits for non-editorial use are not required unless so indicated on the front of the form.

25. **The Illustrator hereby waives the right to injunctive relief for breaches of the right of integrity and the right of paternity.**

Samples

26. Unless otherwise agreed, the Illustrator shall be entitled to receive not less than four proofs or printed copies of the work.

Notices

27. All notices shall be sent to the Illustrator and to the Client at the address stated in this Agreement. Each party shall give written notification of any change of address to the other party prior to the date of such change.

28. These terms and conditions are governed by the law of England and Wales and may not be varied except by agreement in writing. The parties hereto submit to the non-exclusive jurisdiction of the English Courts.

A member of the Association of Illustrators

3 | Notes to the AOI Terms and Conditions

Our aim has been to produce a clear and unequivocal contract between illustrator and client which is fair to both sides. This inevitably leads to a certain amount of compromise, but we think it is in the long term interests of the profession that they should be drafted in this way, both as a matter of principle and in order that they should gain wide acceptance.

3:1 A number of clients have terms and conditions which very effectively protect the client's interest by ignoring those of the illustrator. Competing sets of unfair terms and conditions from illustrator and client add nothing but confusion to the commissioning of illustration, an outcome to be avoided at all cost.

The AOI Terms and Conditions are offered as a model for illustrators to use, or modify, or ignore as they wish. We expect that many agents in particular will want to modify them to suit their particular requirements. However, we would strongly advise members to check any proposed modifications with a solicitor specialising in intellectual property law, as sometimes what seems a simple change of wording can have unexpected implications.

These terms are designed for one-off illustration jobs, and are not adequate where royalty payments are to be made, when illustrators should have a properly drawn up royalty contract.

3:2 When to use the AOI Terms and Conditions

The terms and conditions are a 'job acceptance' form, and should be sent to the client as soon as the commission is agreed and a copy kept by the illustrator. They can be sent by post, fax or email.

It is important to send them as soon as the commission has been agreed. If they are sent at rough stage or later, at artwork stage or invoice stage, they may not be legally binding. (For the reasons for this, see 8:1 – 8:5).

However, even sent at later stages, the use of the terms and conditions tells the client what your understanding of the agreement is and gives him/her a chance to raise any objections so, even though not legally binding, they are worth using at any stage if you have not sent them when the commission was received.

Use of the terms and conditions involves writing a licence for each job by filling in the form at the front, and guidance on writing licences can be found in Section 4.

Notes on the Clauses

3:3 Clause 1

This clause re-states what is in fact the legal situation unless otherwise agreed, and technically hardly needs saying. However it is useful in situations (for instance if the artwork is based on a designer's rough) where the copyright ownership may be unclear.

The only circumstance where an assignment of copyright to the client *may* be appropriate is in the case of a trade mark or company logo.

3:4 Clause 2

Since the fees charged by illustrators vary greatly, according to the use, it is important to define what use has been granted. (See section 5)

3:5 Clause 3

This clause needs to be considered by the illustrator each time a licence is granted. It protects a client, who will have purchased a limited usage, from seeing the image exploited by others in any situation detrimental to the client's business. In some cases – for instance where greetings card rights are being licensed – the illustrator may wish to restrict the clause further by adding 'Clause 3 applies to other exploitation of UK rights only' under 'Special Terms' on the front of the form, thus leaving the illustrator free to exploit foreign rights without having to seek permission from the original client. Or the illustrator may wish to delete it altogether, and be free to sell calendar rights, T-shirt rights, etc in the UK, leaving the client only UK greetings card rights as would be normal in this particular market. Clearly the whole matter should be discussed with the client before the licence is issued.

In advertising or design jobs it may be more appropriate to give the client the absolute right of veto of any other use for a period after the licence has expired.

For guidance, see section 4 'Writing a licence'.

3:6 Clause 4

The client needs to be sure it can make further use of the illustration without the possibility of being held to ransom over the fee. This clause ensures that the illustrator cannot charge more than 'the going rate'. (For more on re-use fees, see Appendix C)

3:7 Clause 5

This clause, known as a *Romalpa Clause*, gives the illustrator important protection if the commissioner uses an image without paying. It can be especially useful if an intermediary (eg a design group) goes bankrupt after being paid by its customer/end-user, but before it has paid the illustrator. In such cases the design group will often set up as a new company under the same name and with the same clients, but having shed its previous debts[1]. Under this clause, since the illustrator has not been paid, no rights have transferred, and the illustrator will have a case for breach of copyright against the customer/end-user, *whether or not the customer has paid the design group*. Very often, in practice, the threat of bringing such a case will be enough to persuade the design group to pay the debt, even though they are not legally bound to, in order to avoid causing trouble with a client they may still be working for.

3:8 Clause 6

In the unlikely event that the client or customer wants to hand on the licence to a third party, the illustrator must have the right to object if the third party is one he/she does not want to be associated with.

3:9 Clause 7

In practice most editorial commissioners pay fairly promptly, whereas advertising and design commissioners are much more tardy. An alternative, and some say more effective way of getting clients to pay in time, is to offer a small discount for payment within one month.

3:10 Clause 8

The reason for charging a cancellation fee before rough stage (when the illustrator may not even have started work) is that in taking on a commission the illustrator will have turned down other work, and may therefore find him/herself unemployed for a period as a result of the cancellation. A *cancellation* (as opposed to a *rejection*) occurs when the project is cancelled through no fault of the illustrator.

3:11 Clause 9

Many advertising jobs are based on a designer's rough which has been approved by the client before the illustrator is approached. Having paid the cancellation fee, the client is entitled to 'keep' its rough image in case it is needed later.

3:12 Clause 10

Delays are sometimes caused by clients, especially when a job has to be approved by a number of different people, and such delays can produce severe knock-on effects for an illustrator with a tight schedule of work. However, the client must have a sanction when the delays are the fault of the illustrator.

3:13 Clause 11

Consequential damages could be large and unforeseeable. The postponement of a major advertising campaign, for instance, may cost the client many thousands of pounds. A similar exclusion clause in favour of the client is to be found in clause 22. Exclusion clauses are in bold type because they need to be brought to the contracting parties' attention to be legally binding.

3:14 Clauses 12,13,14

The whole question of rejection fees is fraught with difficulty. In law, a person who provides goods to order is entitled to their money if the goods are supplied as ordered. This means that an illustrator who works according to the brief and to the standard of the samples in his/her portfolio is entitled to the full fee. But if he/she has made a mess of the job, to no payment at all.

Such a situation is a recipe for endless disputes about highly subjective matters and about contested details of an (often verbal) brief. Hence the idea of a set rejection fee, which has become accepted practice. But some illustrators (particularly agents) and clients have come to regard the rejection fee as negotiable. Logically a negotiable rejection fee takes one back to the original situation: if the client thinks it's all the illustrator's fault, he/she won't want to pay anything, and the illustrator who thinks it's all the client's fault will want paying in full, and we are back to protracted disputes again.

We feel, therefore, that rejection fees should be fixed at 50% *whatever the reason for the rejection*. On a swings and roundabouts principle this should work out fairly in the long run, and save a very great deal of time and hassle.

Clause 12, however, offers some protection to the illustrator against those clients who mysteriously refuse to pay their bills for months and then say they have rejected the artwork. It's an arbitrary clause, but has the advantage of certainty.

Sometimes cancellations are disguised as rejections to avoid the higher cancellation fee. If the project goes ahead with another image, it's a rejection. If not, it's almost certainly a cancellation.

3:15 Clause 15

Most illustrators have the occasional client who changes its mind a lot, and this clause allows the illustrator to make an extra charge if this happens. The last part of this clause protects the illustrator from commissions which change their nature half-way through and become very uncongenial. This situation may happen because an art director has been trying to convert his/her client to an adventurous approach, and finally failed. However, illustrators should not invoke this clause lightly, especially if to do so would leave the client with deadline problems.

3:16 Clause 16

The habit of cropping and, worse, stretching and distorting illustrations to fit a space, seems to have increased of late, perhaps because designers have got used to using stock photography in this way. Some illustrators may wish to strengthen this clause so that they have a veto over such treatment.

3:17 Clause 17

Since the illustrator has no way of knowing where reference material supplied by the client comes from, he/she cannot take responsibility for it. ('warrants' means the same as 'guarantees').

Clause 17 does not specifically *indemnify*[2] the client. The effect of this is that the illustrator is liable for claims against the client which turn out to be justified but is protected from having to bear the expense of defending unsuccessful claims (see also note to Clause 18).

3:18 Clause 18

On the other hand, the client indemnifies the illustrator against the cost of any claims, whether successful or not. This reflects the unequal very financial resources of each party.

3:19 Clause 19

This is in fact the underlying law and generally accepted by clients, but a few clients who are unused to commissioning illustration may be unaware of it.

3:20 Clause 20

This protects the artwork from alteration, but not the reproduced image, which is dealt with in Clause 16.

3:21 Clause 21

Book publishers may need to keep the artwork for longer than six months because of the long production time involved, and it may be appropriate to insert a special term on the front of the licence in such cases.

3:22 Clause 22

The AOI used to recommend that compensation for lost artwork should depend on the fee paid for the job. However, there is no logical connection between a usage fee and the value of the artwork.

Artwork values (as opposed to usage values) are based on what the piece would fetch as a work of art. To give an extreme example, an Ian Pollock illustration used by a small magazine for a fee of £100 may well be worth £500. Conversely, a black and white drawing of a trainer shoe used as part of a national newspaper advertising campaign for a fee of £1,000 may be worth no more than £50 as a piece of art.

The reason for the AOI being the final arbiters of value is that we can call on people with considerable experience of selling original illustration.

3:23 Clause 23

Consequential damages are excluded because they are very uncertain and unforeseeable by the client. See also Clause 11.

3:24 Clause 24

Before the 1989 Copyright Act it was the custom that advertising work was not credited. The 1988 Act, however, gives illustrators a general statutory right (the right of paternity) to be credited for their work, and though there will be instances where the client or the client's customer is unwilling to give a credit, the matter is at least now open to negotiation. Once it has been agreed that a credit is not required, the illustrator cannot subsequently assert the right of paternity, although the issue will be open to renegotiation for any further use of the image. The 'orphan works' issue (see 7:13) makes this a concern.

3:25 Clause 25

It is very unlikely that an illustrator would get an injunction for breach of moral rights, but the mere threat of one could be very damaging, particularly to an advertising campaign. This clause protects the client against such an eventuality. It should be noted that normal cropping, overprinting with type etc is not a breach of the right of integrity. (For a fuller discussion of moral rights, see 7:24).

3:26 Clause 28

Specifying the governing law means that if there is a cross-border dispute, the law of England and Wales prevails.

5 Writing a Licence

the Brief

WHAT
WHEN FOR
WHY
?
?

my artwork

what... if they use it... AGAIN?

But what if it sells millions?

me again

How much?

international? global? national? local?

What if I get it wrong

am... how long will it take... pm

£200 £300 £400?

Happy Birthday

tick tock
12:45

usage GLOBAL or local?
£

Hi!
LOTION

How much?

REMEMBER
AGENT'S FEE

MY ARTWORK!

Packet
Advert
Box
Magazine
CD Book
covers £
CARD
$

International?

What are the term

10% EXTRA
for a rush job?
What did I charge last time

Watch the clause about...

HOW LONG?
...ONE YEAR OR TWO SIR?

look it up

worried

USAGE

BOOK COVERS

TORS BANK 17th Dec.

WORK IT OUT

term

WORK
WORK
WORK

No1

No1

4 Writing a licence

Illustrators normally grant clients a licence for a particular use of their artwork, and the fee charged will vary according to the use purchased.

The object of a written licence is to define the usage right which the client has bought, and to give the client any protection it needs in respect of other uses of the illustration.

4:1 A licence can be limited in any way one chooses, but the most common limits are **use, area, duration** and **exclusivity**. If the client is commissioning on behalf of someone else, the client's customer should be specified.

Use is not often a problem, since the client will usually know what it is commissioning the work for.[1] If further uses are known to be a possibility, but are not being licensed as part of the original licence (eg a brochure cover which the client may later use for a poster) it may be worth stating specifically on the front of the form that further uses will require a further fee, to avoid any possibility of a misunderstanding.

Area or **Territory** is an issue which matters in some types of licence but not others. There is a difference in the fee for instance, for a *UK* advertising campaign and an *international* advertising campaign, so it is important to know what the client wants. Common categories for *area* are UK, Europe, USA, World.

Area is also important where merchandising rights are being sold – for instance an illustrator may want to sell greetings card rights in several different countries to different clients.

In some cases *area* may not be an appropriate definition – for example book jackets, where the publisher will want to use the illustration for their UK edition, which may be distributed not just in the UK but throughout the Commonwealth, and even find it's way into English language bookshops throughout the world.

Duration can be a difficult part of the licence to define. The client may not have given much thought to how long it intends to use the illustration for. In the case of a brochure for a bank for instance, the bank may not be able to say how long they will want to use it. The solution in many cases is to give a long licence. After all, in the bank brochure example, the main purpose of the licence from the illustrator's point of view is to make sure that the image is not used by the bank for any other purpose without payment of an appropriate fee. By the very nature of things, the brochure won't be used forever.

The duration of the licence may need to be considered in connection with Clause 3 of the Model Terms and Conditions, if the client needs exclusivity to last beyond the period of the licence, or if the licence is a very long one.

1. For a way of dealing with clients who are vague about this, see 6:11

2. But be aware – an 'exclusive' licence means that the illustrator cannot herself use the image for the purpose covered by the client's licence. If there is a possible clash, cover this by reserving to yourself the right to use the image for your own promotion.

Exclusivity can be a misleading concept. Often it does not mean totally exclusive to the client, but exclusive only in respect of the licence they have bought. An exclusive licence for use on T-shirts in the UK, for instance, does not prevent the illustrator from licensing the image in other territories, or for other uses. If the client wants no other use to be made of the image at all, this needs to be added as a special term.

An exclusive licence is required by most clients within the limits of the licence they have been granted, and often outside those limits as well. For instance, going back to the bank brochure example, the client may well want to be sure not only that they have exclusive use as a brochure cover, but also that no one else will use the image for any other purpose which would be detrimental to them. The AOI model terms and conditions give this protection in Clause 3.[2]

Here are a few examples of licences for different types of commission, using the format in the AOI Model Terms and Conditions.

4:2 Magazine illustration

Terms of Copyright Licence to be granted:

Use:	Magazine illustration, one use, half-page, colour
Customer:	As above
Area covered by licence:	UK
Exclusive/Non-exclusive:	Exclusive
Duration:	One month from first publication
Special Terms (if any):	First British Serial Rights

Some magazines syndicate artwork (ie sell on the rights to other magazines) or may want to have repeat use of an illustration. An alternative licence to accommodate this might be:

Terms of Copyright Licence to be granted:

Use:	Magazine illustration, one use, half-page, colour
Customer:	As above
Area covered by licence:	World
Exclusive/Non-exclusive:	Exclusive
Duration:	5 years
Special Terms (if any):	Client may syndicate the illustration on an exlusive basis on payment to the illustrator of 50% of syndication fees obtained

4:3 Brochure

Terms of Copyright Licence to be granted:

Use: A4 Cover + 6 quarter-page illustrations for Annual Report and Accounts 1989, colour

Customer: Fat Cat Investments Ltd

Area covered by licence: World

Exclusive/Non-exclusive: Exclusive

Duration: One year

Special Terms (if any):

This assumes that Fat Cat will use the brochure for one year only, but an extra year on the licence would give them a bit of leeway if they are unsure.

4:4 Greetings card

Terms of Copyright Licence to be granted:

Use: Greetings Card illustration, print-run: 10,000

Customer: As above

Area covered by licence: UK only

Exclusive/Non-exclusive: Exclusive

Duration: 2 years

Special Terms (if any): Clause 3 applies in UK only

Such a licence would be suitable if, as is common, no royalties are being paid. At the end of two years (or whatever the duration is) the card manufacturer could, if it wished, renew the licence on payment of a further fee. Licences for tins, T-shirts, calendars, etc would be similar to this if there were no royalty.

See "Notes to Terms and Conditions" for Clause 3 'Special Terms'.

4:5 Book jacket

Terms of Copyright Licence to be granted:

Use: Cover design for (title of book) client's own UK hardback edition only

Customer: As above

Area covered by licence: See 'Use'

Exclusive/Non-exclusive: Exclusive

Duration: As required (or *10 years* or *period of copyright*)

Special Terms (if any): None

Defining on the type of edition on which the illustration is to be used can be important, since if the illustration is used later for a paperback, or for a foreign publisher's edition, the illustrator would expect to get more money.

Some publishers may want to handle such subsequent rights sales themselves, passing on 60-70% of fees obtained to the illustrator.

4:6 Book illustration
Terms of Copyright Licence to be granted:

Use: Half-page colour book illustration only (title of book)

Customer: As above

Area covered by licence: World

Exclusive/Non-exclusive: Exclusive

Duration: Period of copyright

Special Terms (if any): This licence is for volume rights only

This licence would be suitable where the illustrator is making a small contribution to a book for a flat fee – for instance some technical drawings in a 'how-to-do-it' book, or contributions to an educational book.

The important point is to limit the use to books (ie volume rights) so that, should the publisher later decide to branch out into part-works, or make posters for sale, there would be an appropriate payment. Publishers of such a right would normally want world volume rights since sales of foreign editions would be integral to their operation.

Educational books are something of a special case, and may require a special licence.[3]

4:7 Poster
Terms of Copyright Licence to be granted:

Use: 48 sheet poster, colour

Customer: Fruity Beverages Ltd

Area covered by licence: UK

Exclusive/Non-exclusive: Exclusive

Duration: 1 year

Special Terms (if any): Clause 3 applies for 5 years after expiry of licence

Since poster campaigns have to be site-booked and therefore planned in advance, details of area and duration are generally very specific. See note to Clause 3 in "Notes on Terms and Conditions" for 'Special Terms').

4:8 Press advertisement
Terms of Copyright Licence to be granted:

Use: Black and white full-page national newspaper advertisement

Customer: Costa Mucho Holidays Ltd

Area covered by licence: UK

Exclusive/Non-exclusive: Exclusive

Duration: 1 year

Special Terms (if any): Clause 3 applies for 1 year after expiry of licence

---

3. Educational Books.
Really there's no reason why educational books should be licensed any differently from books in general, but in practice it's a sector with horrendous problems. Attempted rights grabs by the publisher are sadly common in this field and though often this is a mere try-on, they can be tedious to negotiate and publishers seem to expect to get very extensive rights. Given that this field is not well paid, illustrators may ask themselves if it's worth bothering with. In practice publishers are likely to insist on a licence for all forms of publication (including electronic), world-wide and for the whole period of copyright. The absolute priority for the artist is to limit the use of the image to the title/project for which it was commissioned, and avoid it being re-used for other things, or worse, re-sold in an image bank. I suggest leaving the licence blank except for 'special terms' –

Special Terms (if any):
In consideration of the payment of (specify the sum) the Illustrator hereby grants to the Publisher the sole and exclusive right and licence to publish and themselves to licence the publication of the Illustrations in connection only with the Work entitled (name of work) or any adaptation or abridgement or substantial part of the Work in volume form for the legal term of copyright throughout the world.

Unfortunately most educational publishers are hung up on getting electronic rights as well, and in practice the illustrator is likely to find (s)he has to grant this, in which case the words 'in volume form' should be altered to 'in any form' and the following should be added:

No licence is granted to the Publisher for publication in any context except that of the original Work for which the illustrations were commissioned and for the avoidance of doubt the Publisher is specifically excluding from using the Illustrations in any image library either for their own use or for licensing to any third party.

You will probably need to put all this on a separate sheet of paper, and write on the form 'see licence attached'.

5 five

SIZE

8	2½'
18	9½'
9	5
4	2
5	3 28
	9—1

USAGE

DURATION

1	8	2½'	
2	8	2½'	
	18	9½'	
1	9	5	
	4	2	
1	5	3 28	
		19—	
1. 5. 3		9	
1			
	1	2½	
	18	9½	

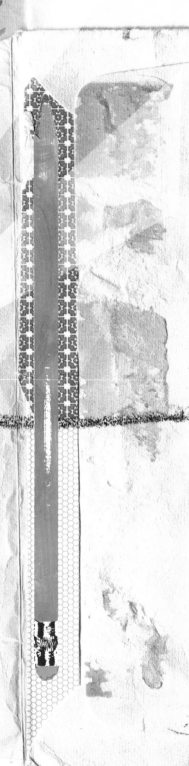

23 | 24 | 25 | 26 | 27 | 28 | 29 | 30

5 | Fees

Fees for illustration vary according to the use to which the image is to be put. This system is quite normal in the visual arts industry as well as in many other fields. Photographers vary their rates in the same way, and so do designers.

5:1 For instance a quarter page illustration might fetch as little as £150 in a low circulation magazine, but around £2000 if it were used for a national newspaper campaign – even more if it were used for an international campaign or trademark.

Most illustrators and agents work out a fee predominantly on the basis of use, sometimes with weighting added for the amount of work involved, the individual illustrator's reputation, a tight deadline, the client's budget and so forth.

A small number of illustrators break fees up into two parts: an hourly rate calculated by estimating how long the job will take, plus an element for the usage. Aside from the difficulty in predicting how long a job will take, the fact is that some jobs will scarcely cover an hourly rate, let alone a usage fee on top. This method of fee calculation is unnecessarily complicated for most people.

Since fees vary so widely according to usage, it follows that clients and illustrators need to be clear what use is being sought and sold, and if the client is acting as an intermediary (as in the case of a design group), the client's customer needs to be made aware of the limits of the licence it has bought.

5:2 How much is it worth?

Any kind of guide to actual fees that illustrators might charge is fraught with difficulties. There is wide variation between small circulation and mass circulation magazines, for instance, and between a logo for your local plumber and a logo for an international company.

In addition, prices quoted here will become out of date with the effects of inflation and changes in the market. Illustrators who are well-known and much in demand may be inclined to charge more than beginners; or the fee may increase to take account of a tight deadline, or be lower for an attractive job.

That being said, what follows is a rough indication for the sake of students fresh from college and clients unaccustomed to commissioning illustration, of the range of fees illustrators currently obtain for different uses. *It should be born in mind that it may be out-of-date when you are reading this guide.*

More detailed (and up-to-date) information can be found in the review of fees which is updated periodically and published by the Association of Illustrators.

Illustration by Sarah Hanson

5:3 Magazines and newspapers

Art directors usually have a set budget for buying in photography and illustration, with limited room for manœvre. The amount seems to vary from periodical to periodical usually, but not always, according to the circulation. A comparison of the amount charged for advertising space with the amount paid to contributors would be very interesting, if anyone had the patience to do it.

All these prices are for one use only.

Covers vary from £500 – £1000.

Inside illustrations less than full page from £150 – £450 depending on published size.

Full page inside illustrations around £450 – £800

5:4 Book covers

Vary from around £400 – £1000 depending on whether it's a modest seller or a mass-market mega seller, for use in the publisher's own edition. Paperbacks are usually better paid than hardbacks.

5:5 Record/Cassette/CD covers

Prices seem to be in the same general range as book covers, with classical music tending to be at the lower end, popular music at the higher.

We sometimes come across illustrators who have done record sleeves for a band at the beginning of its career for next to nothing, and find the work still being used later when the band becomes successful. Record companies – particularly small ones – seem to be particularly inclined to think they can go on re-using an illustration for things like merchandising as often as they like without further payment. All the more important to license clearly in the first place.

5:6 Educational books

Fees seem to range from horrible to reasonable. About £300 – £500 per double page spread seems to be normal. The worst I have ever come across was £50 per page, which is ridiculous.

5:7 Children's picture books

Mostly paid with royalties. If you are the fortunate illustrator of a bestseller on a royalty, you can make your fortune. More usual is to be paid an advance of between £3000 and £5000 (sometimes more). Be aware that the book may not sell enough copies to earn anything more than the advance. A good rule is to work out your minimum acceptable hourly rate, and multiply it by the number of hours you think the book will take. Will the advance cover this sum?

5:8 Greetings cards

This is a horribly underpaid activity. Flat fees are between £150 and £250 per design. Royalties more likely to be offered by smaller companies. We have some anecdotal evidence that royalty payments make more money in the long term, so they may be worth going for if you can.

5:9 Brochures and other 'below-the-line' publicity

Generally commissioned by design groups on behalf of their clients. There is a lot of room for bargaining in this very varied area, which includes brochures, mail-outs, and point of sale material. Typical brochure cover fees would be £400 – £1200 depending on size and print-run. Inside illustrations range from £250 for small vignettes to £1000 for full page. Other below-the-line work (that is to say publicity material which is not media advertising) is so variable that it's hard to give typical fees, but in general it is better paid than magazine work, without reaching the dizzy heights of above-the-line advertising. For more details see the AOI review of fees.

5:10 Packaging

There is huge variation depending on the manufacturer and the size and impact of the image. A small vignette for a frozen fish pack may pay only £250, a wrap around colour pack for tea £1000; more complicated items (eg an Easter Egg) £1500. If the image is used for point of sale, as is often the case, there should be more money.

5:11 Advertising

Generally commissioned by advertising agencies and handled by artists' agents, this is where the largest fees are to be found. Again, there is often much room for bargaining. A typical quarter page black and white newspaper ad might be £600 or so, a full page one £1000 – £2500 depending on client, number of inserts, regional, national or international distribution. Colour illustrations for trade press advertising are in a similar range – more in the public press.

Posters vary enormously according to size and distribution. A poster may fetch £500 if there are to be only one or two on selected sites, or £4000 if it's a national campaign. International campaigns would fetch yet higher prices.

These are just a few examples of typical prices currently being charged. Remember that every bargain is an individual one. The illustrator may ask more, or accept less, than the prices given here.

The National Union of Journalists publishes a set of recommended fees and daily rates for different types of freelance work, including illustration and photography. To get hold of it you need to be a member or know a freelance journalist who is.

5:12 Re-use fees

Clients sometimes want to make additional uses of an image over and above the use they originally commissioned.

There is no generally accepted practice about how to quote for re-use fees. Some illustrators seek to charge the full going rate for re-use, others give a discount of up to 50% (or more if there are a lot of re-uses), especially if the re-use is wanted by the original client.

If you give a discount, be aware that the result can vary depending on whether the original fee was higher or lower in value than the discounted fee. For instance:

Original commission: a brochure cover at full going rate	£1000
Re-use for advertising (going rate £2000) 50% discounted rate	£1000
Total for both uses	£2000

But if these are commissioned the other way around:

Original commission: advertising at full going rate	£2000
Re-use for brochure cover (going rate £1000) 50% discounted rate	£500
Total for both uses	£2500

A solution to this conundrum is to re-calculate the whole bundle of uses, starting with the highest value at the full rate regardless of which was commissioned first.

An even more complicated way of quoting for re-use (only in advertising) was negotiated by the Association of Photographers, the Association of Illustrators and the Advertising Art Buyers Committee. This system produces quite high fees, and whilst it is often used as a starting point (by those who understand it), the re-use figures it produces sometimes have to be modified to take account of the client's budget. Both systems are described in full in Appendix C.

6
NEGOTIATING

6 Negotiating

Many illustrators, myself included, are not especially good negotiators; but unless there's an agent to take the flak, illustrators have to do the best they can. However poor a negotiator you are to start out with, having the right frame of mind, the right manner, a few practical techniques and knowledge of the issues in different sectors of the market will help you get better.

The right frame of mind

6:1 Your client needs you

Being a freelance illustrator can be an insecure existence. If the work's not coming in and the bills need paying it's easy to feel at a disadvantage and overly grateful that someone, somewhere is prepared to pay you to make an image for them.

But remember that, though you may need the work, equally the client needs you. The client has chosen you because he/she needs to get the job done and thinks you are the right person for it. The last thing the client wants is to have to go looking for another, probably second-choice, artist. You may feel that you are competing with all the other illustrators around, but in fact you are not. For any particular job there are only a limited number (sometimes very limited) of suitable artists known to the commissioner. You are in a stronger position than you may think.

6:2 'It's a win-win scenario'

This rather nauseating phrase, beloved of management people, is nevertheless true. The object of a good negotiation is to arrive at a point that is acceptable to both parties, not for one party to screw the other. To do that you need to know not only what *you* need, but also what the client needs.

Faced with a rights grab, for instance, simply saying 'No I won't assign you the copyright' is not a particularly good tactic, since it closes the door on further discussion. A more productive approach is to find out *why* the client wants the copyright and see if you can offer them an alternative that deals with their concerns and is acceptable to you.[1]

In a nutshell, never say 'No', always say 'Yes, but...'

6:3 You are the expert

Or if you're not, you should be. It goes without saying that you're an expert illustrator; but you should also take time out to find out the 'going rate' for a range of jobs so that you have confidence in what you are asking. The AOI publish a review of typical fees periodically.

Illustration by Paul Bommer

1. See, for instance, 'Menu Quotes', 6:11

2. Sadly 'proper' art directors who make their own decisions on the visual aspect of the product are now harder to find in the magazine world.

6 | Negotiating | page 37

Since you are reading this guide, you should also be pretty expert on matters of copyright and the other bits of law that affect illustration, certainly more expert than most of your commissioners. Even commissioners one would expect to know their stuff can be amazingly ignorant. My agent once rang an advertising art buyer to object to a term in the agency's contract only to be asked 'Oh, what's in it? I've never read it.'

I myself was once asked to do a brochure illustration based on the well-known Escher image of an endless water-tower. When I looked up Escher's death date, I found that he was still in copyright and both I, the commissioner and the client could have been in trouble if we'd gone ahead without permission.

It helps to be familiar with different ways of licensing, and be able to explain clearly to a client, if they are asking for copyright or some other right you don't want to grant, *why* you don't want to grant it and what you could offer instead that might work for them.

6:4 Who is commissioning you?

The person you are negotiating with may not be the ultimate decision-maker, in fact usually is not. If it's an editorial job the last word on the suitability of your rough will probably be with the editor[2], and as for copyright issues, the person commissioning, who may be quite a junior designer, may be constrained by fixed company policy. He/she is very unlikely to be responsible for the awful contract you are being offered, and may well be sympathetic to your concerns, so don't treat commissioners as the enemy – try to enlist their support rather than alienate them.

If it's a design or advertising job then the client will have the last word. Designers have a particular difficult time, because unlike advertising agencies, they tend to have short-term relationships with their clients and typically have to pitch for each job. This can make them very nervous of alienating clients, and so hard to negotiate with. Let them know you are aware of the problems and trying to find a solution that they can present to their client, and you may get them on your side.

6:5 Be prepared to lose the job

Lastly, you must know where your bottom line is and be prepared to lose the job if necessary. In my experience it seldom happens, but it sometimes does, usually over money rather than rights. If it does, it may be some consolation to know that in my fairly long experience of advising fellow illustrator for the AOI, clients who offer rotten money or horrible terms (or both) often turn out to be impossible clients in just about every other way as well. They are probably best avoided.

Have the right manner

6:6 Be nice

I have lost count of the number of times an illustrator who has been ripped off by a client says 'But they seemed so nice'. Of course they did. Being nice is a very effective negotiating tactic.

By 'be nice' I don't mean give the other side whatever they want. You should stick to your negotiating aims and be clear what is acceptable to you and what is not. But 'being nice' is all the more important when telling the client something they *don't* want to hear.

As Disraeli famously found when dealing with Queen Victoria, flattery will get you a long way, as will showing an interest in the job and some general enthusiasm. For instance I like best working with design groups (rather than magazines) because the design environment in which the illustration appears is much more likely to be a good one. So if my client sends me a pdf of the page my picture is appearing on, and I think it's a nice piece of typography, I say so. It all helps to oil the wheels.

Above all, never let yourself get angry; never write long ranting letters, whatever the provocation. If you just can't bring yourself to be nice, at least be business-like. Bear in mind you will, with any luck, get more work from the same client; so you need to have a good working relationship.

6:7 Be upfront

It is tempting to try to ignore bad contracts and awkward issues, to hope for the best, or to think it can all be ironed out later. This never works, and if you've read the 'Contracts' section you will know it's usually a disaster legally as well.

If you have an issue with some part of a commission you just have to be upfront about it – in a nice way, of course. Even if I'm thinking 'Why are these bastards messing me about' I find it helps to sound cheerful, even if through gritted teeth.

Some practical tips

6:8 Get as much information as possible

It helps when a call comes through with a possible job to start by finding out as much as possible about the job and the client. You need to know about the deadline for roughs and a/w, the size, and whether the client has a preconceived idea about what they want. It may be relevant to find out what image of yours they've seen, because that's the sort of thing they'll be expecting to get, whatever they say about not having a preconceived idea. Unless it's obvious, you need to ask what they are using the image for. By the time you have discussed all this, you should have established some kind of rapport with the commissioner, and have given yourself time to think about the fee.

6:9 Make notes

It may sound obvious, but it's surprisingly easy to misremember details; so note down the salient points as the conversation goes on. It may also help to have a checklist of questions to ask about a job stuck up near the telephone where you can see it.

6:10 A few useful phrases

Since most commissions come in on the phone without any warning (and often at inconvenient moments), it's handy to have a few stock phrases ready.

If you need time to think (because you've been asked to quote, or for some other reason) say something like 'Can I get back to you in 30 minutes?' The client may well need to get the job commissioned in a hurry, so it's important to say when they can expect a decision. Meanwhile, if you need to, get advice from friends or from the AOI. It will also help to jot down your bottom line, and any points or arguments you want to make when you ring the client back.

Some illustrators are embarrassed to talk about money. So, for that matter, are some commissioners. It's not unknown for a job to be delivered before the fee is discussed. If you are one of these, a stock phrase like 'What's the budget for this?' may be less painful than asking 'How much are you going to pay me?' At least one agent I know is dead against this, taking the view that it's up to the agent or illustrator to set the fee, not the client, but not everyone has that kind of confidence. In any case, the fee mentioned by the commissioner can always be negotiated.

It's always a good idea to express some enthusiasm for the job, even if it's just another 'maze with signposts'. If the client wants 'All Rights' for instance you might say 'It sounds a really interesting job, but I only work on a "One Use" basis'. Or if the fee is too low, 'I'd love to do it, but it's well below my usual hourly rate. Can you squeeze a bit more out of the budget? The (name of rival magazine) usually pay about £x for this sort of job.'

6:11 Menu quotes

The 'menu quote' is a useful way of dealing with demands for copyright assignment or clients who are not sure what rights they want. Instead of quoting just for one particular use you give the client a range of prices for a range of uses.

Suppose you are asked to do a brochure cover, but the client wants copyright, because it feels it may need to use the image for other things, but it's not sure what. Instead of just saying 'No, I don't assign copyright' your 'yes, but' could be a quote as follows:

Brochure cover only:	£1,000.00
All 'below-the-line' uses:	£2,500.00

Advertising use to be negotiated, but typical fees would range from £1,000.00 to £2,500.00 depending on the extent of the advertising.

Complete Copyright:	£8,000.00

This gives the client some choices, whilst making it clear that if they want the copyright they must expect to pay for it. The details of the menu quote would vary according to what uses you think the client is likely to need.

6:12 Re-use prices

This is a minor issue, but annoyingly complicated. Sometimes a client may want a quote for a possible further use. There is no generally agreed method of doing this in the industry, and many illustrators just ask what they think the market will bear. A more logical and fairly common approach is to charge 50% or more of the normal 'going rate' for a re-use by the original client. The same method can be used for working out a quote for a whole bundle of different uses.

The downside of this method is that it produces a different result depending on whether a high-value or low-value use is the first to be commissioned. The only way to overcome this is to bundle all the rights together, charge full price for the highest value use and 50% for the rest. You may find this hard to follow at first reading. If so you are in good company. For a full explanation see Appendix C. It's certainly not easy to explain to a client.

Even harder to understand are the Re-use Guidelines negotiated between the Society of Artists Agents and the Advertising Art Buyers Committee. These, too, are included in Appendix C. They were intended to re-assure advertising clients who said they wanted some predictability in what they would have to pay if they wanted to re-use photography or illustration. They are based on charging a full 'going rate' fee for every use and so tend to produce very high fees, even by advertising standards.

In fact both these methods of calculating re-use fees are chiefly used as a frame-work for working out a fee and for negotiation, rather than a set of hard-and-fast rules. In practice fees for re-use depend as much on the client's budget and what the illustrator is prepared to accept as anything else.

6:13 Client contracts

More clients have standard contracts these days than used to be the case. By no means all do, but if you get one you really *must* read it, or get someone else to. They generally require you to sign and return them and often contain bad news, sometimes hidden in the middle of the contract. Look out for words like 'all rights' and 'buy-out'. They are ways of saying 'copyright assignment' or 'rights grabs'.

If there are bits you don't like, you need to deal with it. Either contact the commissioner and discuss the matter, or simply strike out any offending clauses, initial, and send the contract back, signed, which is what most agents do.

Don't get hung up on inappropriate details. Some issues, like rejection fees, warranties and so forth, are not always vital. It depends on the circumstances. The lack of a rejection fee for a £250.00 magazine job will not be the end of the world; but if the job is a long and highly-priced project, it is very important to make sure rejection and cancellation fees are agreed. Similarly, if you are working with reference supplied by the client, an indemnity from the client really matters. Otherwise it doesn't.[3]

Negotiating issues, sector by sector[4]

6:14 Cards, wraps, stationery, gift-ware etc

Greetings cards are the main part of this market, but it also includes stationery, gift-ware, t-shirts and even the sort of popular prints you see in framing shops. Its trade magazine is *Progressive Greetings* and several trade fairs are held each year in London and Birmingham. There are a few agents who specialise in this field. I have yet to come across one in the UK whose contract I would recommend, though there may be some. They tend to expect to hang on to the right to license anything submitted to them in perpetuity, which is *not* a good idea for the artist. Surprisingly, the contracts I have seen from American agents in this field are a lot better, and since the USA is the biggest market, it may make sense to look for an agent there. Most agents in this field charge 50%.

Like cartooning, you get work in this field by submitting a portfolio of ready-prepared designs. Work is seldom commissioned.

Fees for card designs are typically one-off and not generous. It's a cut-throat business. Clients normally expect to get world rights, and sub-licence to other countries, which is not a good idea if you can avoid it. Try to limit the licence to a particular territory and for no longer than 2 or 3 years (card ranges usually change after this period anyway). Clients also are inclined to ask for Copyright. You should keep the copyright in your image, though they can legitimately claim the copyright in the design of the card as a whole.

Some clients (most commonly the smaller companies) will make royalty deals, and these tend to pay better in the long run. Royalty contracts for cards should last for no longer than 5 years, with the publisher having first right to renew.

6:15 Educational books

There is a good deal of this sort of work about, mostly commissioned by (and art directed by) editors. Fees are one-off and modest. This used to be a quiet backwater of illustration, but is bedevilled these days by publishers trying to get copyright assignments (rights grabs), or failing that, trying to get such an extensive licence that it amounts to the same thing.

It goes without saying that illustrators should avoid assigning copyright[5]. Publishers tend to expect world rights for the period of copyright in all media (including electronic media). It is important to resist this, unless you want to find your work ending up in an image library, possibly sold on to other publishers without any further payment. Illustrators will probably have to give a licence for all forms of publication, but try to confine it to publication *'in the context of the work for which it is commissioned'* and specifically disallow use in an image library. See 4:6f3 for the full wording.

6:16 Children's picture books

The illustrator should expect to get a royalty, usually split 50/50 with the author. Royalty contracts take a lot of negotiating, and there is a full discussion of them in Section 10. It is probably best to get proper advice on a royalty contract (from the AOI or the Society of Authors).

Some smaller publishers and particularly book packagers only offer one-off fees. If this is the case, try to confine the licence to 'the Publisher's own hardback (or paperback) edition only' (See also 4:5) thus ensuring a further payment for foreign or other editions.

You may be asked to do some 'development' work for a proposed project, so that the publisher can see if there is enough international interest to go ahead. If this is the case, make sure you get agreement on the main points of the final contract. It is very unwise ever to do a substantial amount of work on a picture book before the contract has been agreed, and a good publisher would not allow such a situation to arise.

A small number of book packagers are adopting the worst habits of educational publishers and going for a copyright assignment. *Resist at all costs.*

6:17 Children's novels

These are typically illustrated with one picture per chapter in black line. Fees are almost always 'one-off', but the work should be licensed as in 'Book/CD covers etc' below in order to get more money if there are foreign or other editions which use the illustrations.

6:18 Book/CD covers etc

Fees are reasonable in this field, and deadlines usually quite long. It makes no sense to license for a particular period or territory because publishers don't know how long a particular edition will stay in print, and books may find themselves sold in English language bookshops throughout the world. Try to restrict the license to, for instance, 'the Publisher's own hardback edition only', then if the book goes into paperback or it has a foreign edition and the same image is used for the cover (which may well not happen, but sometimes does) you will get a repeat fee.

3. For a full discussion of relevant issues in illustration contracts, see the notes to the AOI Acceptance Form (3).

4. For typical fees in each sector see section 5 (Fees); but bear in mind that they may be out-of-date. The AOI does an updated survey of fees periodically.

5. See also Appendix A 'Rights Grabs' for a full discussion of this issue.

6:19 Magazines and newspapers

Most newspapers and magazines still don't have their own contracts. Those that do should be treated with caution; they are often rights grabs, or All Rights contracts (which is the same thing). They are often presented as the commissioner's 'standard' contract. With a very few exceptions, magazines and newspapers will accept a 'One Use' contract. *You have only to ask.* Fees can be negotiated to a certain extent, but commissioners tend to be quite constrained by a set budget per issue. Never any harm in trying.

6:20 Below-the-line advertising

A mysterious term which simply means advertising when the advertiser is not renting the space. Packaging, point-of-sale, mail-shots, company reports and brochures are all 'below-the-line'. Posters, magazine and newspaper ads and TV ads are 'above-the-line'. Below-the-line work is often commissioned by design groups and includes a huge variety of uses and prices, as well as licences. This sort of work can sometimes be the hardest to negotiate, and fees can vary a lot. A few design groups will try to get copyright, but most are still reasonable. This is a field where the illustrator's agent really comes into his own. The Advertising Art Buyers' Committee Re-use Guidelines (Appendix Section15) may give you an idea of comparative below-the line fees.

6:21 Above-the-line advertising

Nearly always commissioned by specialist art buyers in advertising agencies, this used to be a fraught field for negotiation but has become easier since the introduction of the Advertising Art Buyers' Committee Guidelines published jointly by the IPA (ad agencies' organisation) and ISBA (their clients' organisation). Copyright is seldom an issue, but fees can be quite intricate and in some cases very high. As with below-the-line work, best negotiated by agents. Or get advice. This area can be very well paid.

'7

CopyRight

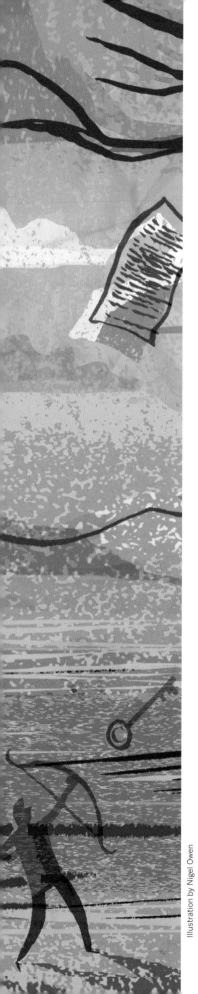

7 Copyright

Copyright is the illustrator's trade. There is sometimes misunderstanding about the meaning of 'copyright' among illustrators and clients. As a result clients ask for ownership of copyright from illustrators without realising just what a very substantial and wide-ranging right it is. This section explains just what copyright is and why in almost all cases a *licence*, rather than a buy-out of copyright itself, is what the client needs when commissioning illustration.

7:1 What is copyright?

'Copyright' is a splendidly simple legal term, because it means exactly what it says. It is the *right* to *copy* something. The owner of the copyright in an image is the only person with the right to copy that image or to allow others to copy it and this applies to any sort of copying – copying by hand[1], copying photographically, making a photocopy or scanning into a computer[2] but, most importantly for illustrators, it applies to copying by reproduction in print or in other media.

'Copyright' is a piece of property just like a car, a house or a washing machine. It is a separate property from the physical artwork. As soon as an artist makes a drawing he/she owns both the *artwork* and the *copyright*,[3] so that it is perfectly possible for an artist to sell an original artwork (the physical property) but still own the copyright in it (the intellectual property), or for an illustrator to sell the copyright but still own the original artwork. (See Appendix G). Like any other piece of property, copyright can be sold, given away, left in a will, or otherwise disposed of.

7:2 Copyright is created as soon as a person puts pencil to paper. Anyone who makes a doodle, takes a photograph, writes a letter, or paints a picture (regardless of its quality) automatically owns the copyright in that doodle, photograph, letter or painting, provided it is *original* in the sense of not itself being a copy of someone else's work, provided it is not 'commonplace'[4] and provided they are not an employee. (Illustrators are nearly always freelance, and therefore not employees; though be aware that you might be an employee, even if you contract says 'freelance', if you do all your work on company premises or are paid PAYE). There is no need to register copyright, to use the © sign or to go through any other formality to establish ownership of the copyright.[5]

7:3 The copyright, once created, will last for the creator's lifetime plus seventy years[6]; so a copyright created by a twenty-year-old illustrator who lives into her eighties might have a life of 120 years or so, after which the work enters the public domain and can be reproduced by anyone. At this point it is said to be *out of copyright*.

7:4 What copyright won't help with

There is no copyright in an *idea*, only in the form the idea takes. If you have a brilliant idea for an illustration and someone copies your idea but renders it in their own distinctive way, they will not be infringing your copyright. However if they copy a substantial part of your actual design, they will be infringing.[7]

Neither is there any copyright in *style*, a fact that seems particularly unfair to the many illustrators whose 'style' is very personal and an important selling point. However, there it is. The only consolation is that illustrators who copy someone else's style are generally frowned on by their colleagues and seldom thrive (though an action for 'passing off' is a remote possibility. See 7:23).

Copyright will not help with similarities that happen by chance. I may produce an image that looks just like one of yours, but if I've never seen yours and haven't copied it, there is no infringement.

7:5 Permitted Acts and Fair Dealing

There are some situations in which copying *is* allowed without permission of the copyright owner and without payment, though the copyright owner should still be credited in some cases. These exceptions to the general rule are known as 'Fair Dealing' and 'Permitted Acts'[8]. They are:

Reporting news or current events For instance when Edvard Munch's *Scream* was stolen it could be reproduced as part of a news report, even though it is still in copyright.[9]

Criticism or review It is permissible to reproduce an image as part of a criticism or review of it or another work. Quite how far this right extends has yet to be properly tested in the courts. A number of art book publishers have in the past relied on it to justify not paying for reproducing works of art, but are now having second thoughts. A book that is primarily a work of criticism is probably safe; a book that is primarily a 'coffee table' book, whose selling point is the pictures themselves, is almost certainly not.

Research and private study, not for profit A person may make one copy of a work for research and private study. To this was recently added (via an EU directive) the proviso that the research and private study must be 'not for profit'– so students are OK, authors and illustrators probably not.

Works on public display Sculptures, buildings and 'works of artistic craftsmanship' which are situated in a public place or a place open to the public may be copied. The meaning of 'works of artistic craftsmanship' is a bit fuzzy, but it does *not* include paintings, drawings and photographs (which are called 'graphic works' in copyright-law-speak).

Advertising works of art for sale It's OK to reproduce a work of art to advertise its sale – in a sales catalogue, for instance. But flogging off your old catalogues after the sale has taken place would be a infringement of copyright.

Subsequent works by the same artist An illustrator may 'copy' an earlier work of which he/she is no longer the copyright owner, provided 'he does not repeat or imitate the main design of the work.' I think this means you can copy a 'substantial part' of one of your own works and it's still OK as long as the 'main

1. Thus when Glen Brown was nominated for the Turner prize for his painting The Loves of Shepherds (After Double Star by Tony Roberts) which was based on Tony Roberts' science fiction paperback cover illustration, the illustrator claimed for infringement of copyright. In this case it has been suggested (by Stuart Lockyear in Dear Images: Art, Copyright and Culture Ridinghouse, 2002) that Glen Brown has a 'fair dealing' defence, as the painting was a 'criticism or review' of the earlier work (see 7:5 below). However, this defence was greatly weakened by the fact that Glen Brown did not originally acknowledge the source of his painting. This case was settled out of court.

2. Before you get too excited at the thought of all those clients scanning your work into their computers without permission, bear in mind that they will often be covered by an implied license (See 8:8 et seq), and unless they are then disseminating your images on the web or on an intranet it's not worth suing them anyway. (See 7:9 - 'penalties for copyright infringement').

3. Provided the artist is not an employee, in which case the employer is the first owner of the copyright.

4. This may well apply to, for instance, stick men, or a simple icon of a house drawn in the way a child would draw it.

5. Though if it's very important to be able to prove that a work was created at a certain date it may be worth sealing a copy of the work, posting it to yourself and keeping it unopened so that the postmark gives evidence of the date of creation. Such elaborate precautions are hardly ever necessary, however. (See 8:6 'Proof in criminal and civil law'.)

6. From the end of the calendar year in which the creator died.

7. For a rather unsatisfactory protection for ideas, see 7:22.

8. *Fair Dealing* is a defence against an action for what would otherwise be an infringement. A *Permitted Act* is not an infringement in the first place.

9. This applies to illustration and most copyright works, but not to photographs; presumably to give protection to news photographers.

design' is not copied. Hmm. Clear as mud. Best policy is not to let go of the copyright in the first place.

Incidental inclusion 'Incidental' inclusion is allowed, but the meaning of 'incidental' can be unclear. If you draw or photograph a room which *happens* to have a work of art in it, your copying of that work of art is permitted, because it is 'incidentally' included. If you put the work of art there yourself (for instance if you were setting up a scene to draw or photograph), or if you intend the work of art to be a part of your photograph, the inclusion would not be 'incidental' and would not be a permitted act.

7:6 Infringing copyright

It is often difficult to be certain whether something is or is not an infringement of copyright. The line between the two can be annoyingly fuzzy, and will depend on the particular facts of the case and the (sometimes idiosyncratic) judgment of a court. The basic test is that if you take a 'substantial' part of someone else's work and use it in your own, then it will be an infringement. The meaning of 'substantial' can also be a bit of a moveable feast. The lips of the Mona Lisa, for instance, are probably a 'substantial' part of that work (because they are so characteristic of it), even though physically they are only a small part of the whole painting. (Since Leonardo is long out of copyright, her lips can in fact be reproduced freely.)

This basic test was extended in the case of *Bauman v Fussell [1953]*. Bauman was a photographer whose picture of a cockfight was published in Picture Post. Michael Fussell was an expressionist painter who based a painting on Bauman's photograph. Bauman sued for copyright infringement. The composition of the painting was the same as that of the photograph, but the colours were described as 'heightened' and, judging from other works by Fussell, the general style would have been expressionist rather than realistic.

The judgment laid down that as well as the test 'has an substantial part of the image been taken?' it is also relevant to ask 'has the feeling and artistic character of the work been taken?' when deciding whether or not there has been a breach of copyright, or can it rather be said that 'he has used the work as an inspiration; he has not copied it but has made a new work of his own'? Commenting on this in *Spectravest Inc v Aperknit [1988]* Millet J said, 'A man may use another's work as inspiration to make a new work of his own, treating the same theme in his own manner; but he is not entitled to steal its essential features and substance and retain them with minor or inconsequential alterations.'

Since copyright is a property, infringement of copyright is theft, and can be prosecuted under the criminal law.[10] I find it useful to think of a copyright infringement in this way, and when in doubt ask myself 'Am I taking someone else's copyright work, the product of their thought and labour, and appropriating it as my own?'

It is particularly important for illustrators to steer well clear of possible copyright infringements because, though nine times out of ten nothing will happen, that tenth time can become a very serious problem indeed. The penalties for copyright infringement can be severe, and the client may well look to the illustrator for compensation if they themselves suffer financially from the infringement.

There are two situations where illustrators may find themselves in particular danger of infringing the copyright of others – using reference, and making collages.

7:7 Reference

Illustrators use reference material all the time, and a lot of it is still in copyright. Don't forget that photographers have copyright in their work in just the same way as illustrators. Just because you have made a loose colour rendering of a black and white photograph perhaps reversed the image left to right and changed the odd detail, this will not necessarily mean there is no infringement. If you have taken a substantial part of the photographer's image and reproduced it as your own, you are likely to be infringing. The rule is to use the information in the photograph, or in a range of photographs, but not to reproduce too much of any individual image. (See case study 4 at 7:31).

7:8 Collage

Collage is another grey and untested area. Of course you are safe using out-of-copyright material; with material that may be in copyright, the standard rule applies: don't use a 'substantial' part of someone else's work or, if you do, get permission from the copyright owner. Extreme distortion of a photographic image in the hope that it will no longer be a 'copy' is a possible way out, but may land the collagist with a charge of infringement of the 'moral right' of integrity (see below). I would be especially wary about using collage in advertising, and make sure that anything suspect is copyright cleared, because people are much more likely to sue for an ad than they are for, say, an editorial illustration.

A related problem with collages is that you may yourself have difficulties litigating to protect the copyright in your collage if it contains, even with permission, a number of other copyright works. This problem of 'embedded copyrights' exists, for instance, in the case of Peter Blake's well-known *Sergeant Pepper* album cover.

If this all sounds a bit grim for collagists, there is some good news. To the best of my knowledge there has been no reported case so far in which a collagist has been sued for a copyright infringement.

7:9 Penalties for infringement of copyright

As the injured party, the copyright owner can expect to be awarded damages set at a sum based on the amount he/she would have been paid for an appropriate licence. In addition to this, the court may award additional damages for 'flagrancy' (ie if the infringer did it knowingly), an injunction to prevent the copying from continuing, an account of profits (the infringer has to pay over any profits they have made from the work) and, perhaps the most powerful weapon of all, an order for 'delivery up' of the infringing copies for destruction.

A case for infringement can be brought against anyone involved, whether they are involved knowingly or not. If an illustrator infringes someone else's copyright, the copyright owner can sue the illustrator and the illustrator's client. If the client can show that they were innocent and did not know there had been an infringement, the court will not award flagrancy damages against them, but may still give an order for 'delivery up'. Should this happen the client may well look to the illustrator for compensation. However it will not come to this. Paying over the going-rate licence fee will usually settle the matter.

Most cases where an illustrator's work has been infringed occur when the client has used the work for purposes beyond the original licence, and in such cases a settlement for damages (an appropriate license fee) and perhaps additional damages if the deed was done knowingly would be expected. However, in a case

10. Criminal law is usually used against people selling pirated CDs or DVDs, and rarely for the sort of copyright infringements illustrators get involved in, which are generally dealt with under civil law. However, not long ago the entire board of directors of a publishing company was prosecuted under criminal law because, it was alleged, they had not paid copyright fees for fine art images they reproduced in some of their books. The ploy was not entirely successful, since criminal law requires a much higher standard of proof, and at that time allowed the defendant to use an 'ambush' defence. For more on proof in criminal/civil law see 8:6.

where the infringer has simply appropriated an illustrator's work without any kind of permission, and especially if they have reproduced it in a way offensive to the illustrator, an injunction to stop and order for delivery up may be appropriate.

7:10 Passing rights to the client
Licences
In the great majority of cases a licence is the most appropriate way for an illustrator to give the client the rights it needs. The illustrator keeps the copyright, and grants the client a licence – or 'permission' – to reproduce the image in a way appropriate to the commission. The licence can be restricted in any way that suits both parties, but would typically state the use (eg 'as a brochure cover'), the territory (eg 'UK only') and the period (eg 'One Year'). The fee would be negotiated on the basis of this particular set of restrictions. The vast majority of illustration and photography is commissioned on the basis of a licence, and the subject is covered in the detail it deserves in the section 4.

7:11 Partial assignments of copyright
A seldom-used alternative to granting a licence is to transfer *part* of the copyright itself, with limitations as to use, period and territory just like a licence. In the past this had one advantage. It gave the commissioner the ability to sue in his own name, whereas if he had an exclusive licence he would have to join the name of the copyright owner to any action for breach of copyright. However, exclusive licensees (which almost all licensed clients are) are now able to sue under their own names, so the reason for this form of transfer has disappeared. Even before 1988 it was hardly used.

7:12 Full copyright assignments
It is almost never appropriate for an illustrator to assign complete copyright to a client; in fact it is very much against the illustrator's interest.

As we have seen, the owner of the copyright is the only person with the right to reproduce an image or to allow others to reproduce it. Thus a client who acquires an 'assignment of copyright' becomes the new copyright owner and has the exclusive right to reproduce the image in any way the client pleases throughout the world and for the whole period of copyright (which may be more than one hundred years, depending on how long the illustrator lives). Worse, once having parted with the copyright, the illustrator herself will no longer have any right to reproduce the image, and if she does so (in the form of artists' cards or in illustration annuals, for instance), she will be infringing the client's copyright. The illustrator will also lose any control over the re-selling of the image, and may find it is sold on to an image bank for royalty-free stock.

Then there's the question of money. Illustrators are paid according to 'use'. An image commissioned for a brochure cover will attract a higher fee than one commissioned for a magazine, for instance; a yet higher fee would be paid for advertising use. It follows that complete copyright, giving unlimited rights of reproduction, should necessarily attract a very high fee indeed.

Clearly a client commissioning a brochure cover does not require any such a wide-ranging right as complete copyright, and certainly would not want to pay the appropriate usage fee. In fact, almost the only instance where a transfer of complete copyright *may* be appropriate is that of a trademark or company logo, and even then it is not necessary. Nevertheless, attempts by some clients to use their bargaining power to 'grab' copyrights are currently a serious threat to illustrators that has to be resisted. (See Appendix A *Rights Grabs*).

Copyright miscellany

Under this heading I include, in no particular order, a collection of minor copyright issues that have in common only that they frequently turn up in the practice of illustration.

7:13 Trade marks

As a general rule it's OK to include trade marks as, say, part of a street scene, provided the context is not libellous. But be especially careful about using trade marks in advertising jobs (in fact, best avoid it, unless it's the client's).

In more detail, trade marks are protected in two ways; by trade mark protection (provided the mark is registered, which most are) and by ordinary copyright. Trade mark protection protects against use of an identical or similar mark by any company in the same line of business and also against any company *in whatever line of business*, in the course of their business, if the use 'takes unfair advantage of or is detrimental to the distinctive character or repute of the trade mark'. Copyright protection will operate in the same way as usual, except that the owner of the copyright is likely to be the company that owns the mark, rather than the designer/illustrator.

7:13:1 Orphan works

'Orphan works' are those works who's copyright owner cannot be identified or cannot be traced. At the time of writing these cannot be reproduced (because permission cannot be sought). Quite reasonable and well-regulated legislation exists to deal with this problem in Canada, but in the USA legislation has been seriously proposed (by the US Copyright Office) which would be highly damaging to illustrators and all other creators, since it would act as an incentive for publishers and aggregators to declare works 'orphan' after only cursory enquiries, and there's nothing much the creator could do about it. Under this proposal once declared 'orphan', a work can be freely used by anybody, and in practice all the creator can do is ask for an appropriate fee (if he/she spots it) and the only way of enforcing this is through the courts. In most cases the cost of litigation would far outweigh any benefit, so in effect the user can dictate the fee it wants to pay. This legislation, if passed, would affect everyone, not just US creators.

Orphan works legislation was proposed in the UK Gowers Report (see 7/16f) and, whilst more likely to follow the Canadian model, will probably be introduced over the next few years.

Because of this, especially the threatened USA legislation, illustrators would now be well advised to seek a credit *wherever possible*. This should not be too difficult for below-the-line work, but may be more problematic for above-the-line advertising.

7:14 Photographs of artwork

It is currently accepted in the UK (though perhaps on rather shaky ground) that a person who makes a slide or photograph of a painting owns the copyright in that slide or photograph (though not, of course, in the painting). Thus if you have a slide made of one of your illustrations, the slide will have two copyright owners – yourself (because you did the painting) and the photographer, who owns the 'photographic' copyright, and in order to reproduce *from the slide* you would strictly speaking need to have the consent of the photographer as owner of the copyright in the slide. On this basis image libraries can claim 'photographic copyright' in their slides of works of art that are themselves out of copyright. This claim was overturned in the USA, but some lawyers think the USA case was wrongly decided, and it is still accepted in the UK where, anyway, the USA decision would not be a binding precedent. At any rate there is no doubt that photographers have copyright in photographs of three-dimensional images. The safest thing for the illustrator is to get an assignment of copyright from the photographer who photographs her image, or permission to use the photographs freely

7:15 Illustrations based on a designer's rough
Designer's roughs are particularly common in advertising, and can sometimes even imitate the illustrator's style and be disconcertingly well executed. In the course of a court case between an illustrator and a commissioning design group the defendants (the design group) said that as the illustration in question had been based on their rough they owned the copyright in it, and the illustrator had no copyright in the finished artwork at all. The judge dismissed this argument, but it does appear that in such a case there would again be what amounts to a joint copyright ownership in the final artwork.[11] Technically, therefore, the illustrator should seek the agreement of the designer before reproducing such artwork in, say, an illustration annual. In practice designers are unlikely to make a fuss in such circumstances. This problem is overcome if the illustrator uses the AOI Acceptance of Commission Form, which states, as part of the agreement, that the illustrator owns the copyright in the final artwork.

7:16 Parody
This is another grey area. It would seem that a parody that is critical of its original can be viewed as a visual form of 'criticism or review' and therefore a 'permitted act', but an uncritical parody, or 'mere pastiche' may not be. So if you are pastiching an in-copyright work it is best to get permission, or make enough changes to be safe. Even in pastiching out-of-copyright works, as is often done in cartoons, it is the convention to acknowledge the original creator.[12]

7:17 'Assignment of copyright must be in writing'
This is perfectly true, but can lead illustrators up the garden path. If you agree to assign copyright, whether verbally or by implication, but haven't put anything in writing, it is true that the copyright has not been assigned. But you can be compelled to carry out what you have agreed to, and put it in writing. (For more on this trap for the unwary see 8:10).

7:18 Copyright before 1988
A work created before 1988 is subject to the previous (1956) Copyright Act. So far as illustrators are concerned the significant differences are:

1. in the case of *commissioned portraits* the copyright belongs to the commissioner unless otherwise agreed;

2. in the case of 'engravings' – by which is meant any kind of print except photographs – the copyright belongs to the commissioner unless otherwise agreed;

3. in the case of works commissioned by the Crown (which includes a government department) the copyright belongs to the Crown unless otherwise agreed and

4. in the case of commissioned photographs, again the commissioner owns the copyright unless otherwise agreed (which means that if you are looking to find the copyright owner of a photograph of that period, it may well be the publisher, not the photographer).

7:19 Employed illustrators and 'work-for-hire'

An illustrator who is a full or part-time employee – (test: if your employer is paying you by PAYE, then you are an employee. If you are working on your client's premises you may be) – does not own the copyright in works created as part of that employment. The employer does, unless otherwise agreed. Almost all illustrators are freelance, so it doesn't apply, but in the USA there is a further pernicious twist to this principle known as 'work-for-hire'. If the freelance illustrator agrees to a contract containing these dread words, or words like them, the commissioner will own the copyright (except under UK law where the concept is not recognised). I have seen the phrase in at least one UK contract, despite the fact that it has no legal force in the UK.

7:20 Privacy and model releases

If you draw a person sitting on a park bench without their knowledge, and subsequently publish the result, they will have redress only if your drawing has defamed them in some way (eg because they were appearing to endorse some product, or because it shows them in an unflattering enough light to be libellous). The drawing must, of course, be a recognisable likeness. So if a picture with a likeness in it is to be used for advertising or promotion it is essential to get the permission of the model (a 'model release'), and the client may want to have a copy[13]. Like illustrators, professional models usually charge fees commensurate with usage. Thus if you have an agreement to use a model for UK publication only, and then need to use the image worldwide, you, or more likely the advertising agency, will owe the model more money. In the case of an advertising job, you will probably be able to get the Art Buyer to organise this.

7:21 Buildings

Included because it has been asked. There is no copyright in buildings in the UK (though there is in their plans and architectural drawings).

7:22 Protecting ideas: 'constructive trust'

Though copyright law does not protect ideas, in some circumstances the law of 'constructive trust' may do so, at least in theory. The idea is that if you tell someone something in confidence, that makes them a trustee of your 'in confidence' information, with a trustee's duty of care. So if you write to a games manufacturer with an idea for a new game, and head your letter 'in confidence', you will in theory avoid the manufacturer pinching your idea, because it will have a trustee's duty of care. In fact games manufacturers and the like usually refuse to accept 'in confidence' information, claiming that most ideas are not new, and they may well be working on something similar themselves.

Another possible strategy for protecting an idea is to use a contract. Send a letter saying 'I have an idea for a new game I would like to disclose to you. Please confirm that if you use it you will pay me reasonable compensation based on current industry rates.' Again it is quite likely the recipient will not be willing to agree to this. The best bet is probably to take your idea to a well-established company with a good reputation, who will hopefully be less likely to rip you off.

11. To be absolutely accurate, the designer owns the copyright in his rough, and the illustrator can copy it because she has the designer's permission. The illustrator owns the copyright in her artwork, but because any third party lacks permission from the designer to reproduce the designer's 'embedded' copyright, this would require permission from the designer to license it to anyone else.

12. The recent Gowers Report on intellectual property has recommended that the government should introduce a specific defence of 'parody' to copyright infringement.

13. It is also advisable to get a model release if the picture is to be used abroad as some countries, like the USA, have 'image rights' which prevent the use of a person's image without their permission.

7:23 Protecting styles: 'passing off'

Like ideas, styles are not protected by copyright. It is sometimes suggested that a claim for 'passing off' might succeed in place of copyright. An action for 'passing off' is essentially about deception – 'Nobody has the right to represent his goods as the goods of someone else'.[14] For such a case to succeed, it seems to me the claimant would have to show that the imitator's actions were likely to make clients think the work was the claimant's, thus causing damage or injury to the claimant's business or goodwill. Thus a prominent credit or signature, showing whose work it is, should be a protection. (The test used by lawyers is known as the 'moron in a hurry' test: it must be clear to the 'moron in a hurry' who the creator of the illustration was). This test may be appropriate for illustrators whose work is bought directly by the public, but in the case of illustrators whose living depends on their reputation among art directors, perhaps a 'moron in the art-room' test would be more appropriate. See also 7:29 *False attribution of authorship*.

7:24 Moral rights

The 1988 Copyright Act introduced two new 'moral rights' to the UK, bringing us into line with the Berne Convention[15] and with what has been the practice in the rest of Europe for many years. Moral rights apply to all creators – writers, photographers, illustrators, composers and creators of 'works of artistic craftsmanship'. They belong to the original creator even if he/she has parted with the copyright, they last for the period of copyright, and can be asserted only by the original creator or his/her heirs. Having said that, they are of little practical importance to many illustrators, not least because, as usual, the UK government of the day watered them down so much when introducing them into UK law as to make them more or less useless. Illustrators may be asked to 'waive' (renounce) their moral rights, usually combined with a demand for copyright assignment, and should resist. However the AOI Acceptance of Commission does waive the right to 'injunctive relief' for breach of moral rights for reasons described below. The two new moral rights are:

7:25 The right of integrity

This is the creator's right to prevent her image being altered in a derogatory and damaging fashion. When the new Copyright Designs and Patents Act came in on 1st August 1989, advertising agencies in particular were alarmed that it might prevent them cropping or over-printing with type and so forth. In fact the Act only prevents treatment which is unusual and not reasonably to be expected – so normal cropping and over-printing is allowed. It is therefore of little practical importance to advertising illustrators, and continental experience has been that even where damage has been proved, compensation has generally been modest.

It is possible for creators to 'waive' the right of integrity, though for the reasons given above there is no reason from the client's point of view why such a waiver should be necessary.

7:26 The right of paternity

This is the creator's right to a credit. In order to become operative the right must be 'asserted', generally 'by instrument in writing'.[16] In practice this seems to mean that it must be asserted at the time a contract is made with the commissioner. Although a later assertion will not be invalid, the courts would be required to take the lateness into account in deciding whether to grant an injunction or award compensation for breach of the right.

14. Lord Halsbury in a classic case on passing off, *Reddway v Banham* (1896)

15. The international treaty setting minimal standards of copyright protection in individual countries.

16. For an example of an assertion, look on the copyright page (usually after the title page) of any book, where you will find the author's right of paternity formally asserted. Wording varies from publisher to publisher.

Like the right of integrity, the right of paternity can be waived and many advertising agencies demand such waivers, fearing that late assertions whilst a campaign is running may lead to injunctions, that their advertising campaigns may end up covered in credits, or that their customers will object to credits being given to illustrators and photographers. These fears are in our view greatly exaggerated. The AOI take the view that the matter is best dealt with, for the time being, by an ordinary contractual agreement about credits, and provisions for this are included in the Model Terms and Conditions, without assertion or waiver of the right of paternity. The existence of this statutory right does, however, strengthen the illustrator's hand in negotiating for a credit in above and below-the-line advertising work.

7:27 Newspapers, magazines and works of reference

The one area in which the new moral rights might be of some use is in newspapers and magazines, where it is usual for illustrators to be credited, and where distortions and changes to the illustrators work sometimes happen, thanks to the wonders of Photoshop. It is ironic, then, that these moral rights do *not* apply to publication in newspapers and magazines or 'works of reference' because of successful pressure applied by newspaper and magazine proprietors fearing complications with sub-editing contributions from journalists.

So far as the right of paternity is concerned, this leaves illustrators in the curious position that the Act gives the right to a credit in advertising work, provided it is asserted, but not in editorial work, a reversal of the normal custom which is exactly the other way round. It should, however, be emphasised that the Act does not prevent illustrators and writers being credited in editorial work; it merely refrains from making such credits a statutory right. Illustrators should therefore require a credit in editorial work as before and ideally have a clause in their terms of trade preventing alteration of an illustration without consent.

7:28 Injunctions for infringement of moral rights

The remedies for an infringement of moral rights are compensation (only likely to be awarded if the illustrator can show financial damage resulting from the breach) and an injunction (court order) to prevent future breaches or to cease the current infringement. Fears have been expressed by the advertising agencies about the possibility that injunctions for breaches of moral rights might bring an advertising campaign to a halt, causing immense damage. In practice it is very unlikely indeed that such an injunction would be granted, but since the mere threat of it could damage the agency's relationship with its client, it seems reasonable for clients to request a waiver of the right to injunctive relief for breach of moral rights, especially as the illustrator is giving up something which she has almost no chance of getting anyway. Such a waiver is included in the AOI Model Terms and Conditions.

7:29 False attribution of authorship

Under the old Copyright Act (1956) creators had a remedy if authorship of a work was falsely attributed to them, and this right is carried over into the 1988 Act and grouped with the other moral rights. The only case I know of in which an illustrator used the right concerned a well-known cartoonist who had assigned his copyright in a cartoon, and found it was being used in an advertising campaign. The original cartoon was a black line drawing, but the advertisers had coloured it in and left his signature on it. He successfully took them to court claiming that the coloured version was not his work, so the 'attribution of authorship' was false. If they had taken his signature off, he would have had no case.

7:30 Resale right (Droit de Suite)

At the time of writing this moral right has just been introduced into UK law for living artists, and may be introduced in 2010 for dead artists.[17] It is the right to a royalty payment every time an artist's original artwork is sold on above a value of 1000 Euros). The current rate is 4% at the lower end, falling to less than 1% as the price of the artwork goes up. Payments capped at a maximum €12,500. This will be an additional source of income for many fine artists and a few illustrators whose originals change hands at a good price. The principal visual arts collecting society administering this right for artists is DACS (The Design and Artist's Copyright Society), a not-for-profit organisation with a substantial number of visual creators on its governing board.

7:31 Case studies in copyright infringement

When clients and illustrators infringe copyright it is usually from carelessness (sometimes willful carelessness) or ignorance. Here are a few typical scenarios, all real life cases.

1. A publisher saw an illustration in *Contact* source book which was perfect for what they wanted. They phoned the illustrator and asked 'Can they use it?' The illustrator said no, because it was already in use in the book for which it was commissioned. So they asked her to do them a new illustration by the end of the week. 'Sorry,' said the illustrator, 'I'm too busy.'

The publisher then phoned a second illustrator with a similar style, showed her the image from *Contact* and asked for something similar, which the second illustrator did. The result, though not identical to the original image in *Contact*, was near enough to cause the original illustrator to feel that her copyright has been infringed and to be generally aggrieved. She threatened to sue, and the publisher eventually paid modest compensation.

2. A publisher commissioned a book jacket illustration, which went through to artwork without any problems. Then the author saw it, didn't like the illustrator's style and, since the author was a big seller and could throw her weight about, the publisher reluctantly paid a 50% rejection fee to the original illustrator, commissioned someone else, and presumably showed the second illustrator the original illustration.

As in the previous example, the second image was very like the first in composition, though the styles were slightly different. The first illustrator threatened to sue, but the publisher claimed that the close similarity in the composition of the pictures was a coincidence, the result of a very tight, prescriptive brief, and not a copy.

What gave the game away, though, was that the heroine was depicted in both images wearing a cloak with identical folds, a result which is very unlikely to have come about by chance. Once again, the publisher paid compensation.

The lesson for clients from both these cases is that when re-commissioning a work it is best not to show the second illustrator the original image; and for illustrators to be wary of these situations and make sure their new image is substantially different from the original one. In both the above cases, had the infringed illustrator been angry enough, he could have asked for an order for 'rendering up' (7:9).

17. In which case it will last until the copyright expires.

18. Which gives the agent's contract precedence. See 8:15 'The battle of the forms'.

3. A design group commissioned an illustrator through his agent to make 'presentation roughs' for a logo for their client, who we shall call 'Company A'. (A licence for 'presentation roughs' means that the design group has the right to use the roughs to 'present' for Company A's approval, but not for any other purpose, and the fee is appropriately modest. If Company A gives approval and the job goes ahead, a new fee would be negotiated for the actual logo artwork.)

The logo was to show a formalized image of an owl. The roughs (four of them) were submitted and presented to Company A, but disappointingly the design group rang to say that they have decided not to use them for the logo.

By sheer chance two weeks later 'Company B' rang the same agent wanting the same artist to design a logo for them, also featuring an owl. 'As it happens,' said the agent, 'our artist has just done some owl images which are not going to be used. Would you like to see them?' Company B agreed, the roughs were submitted and, after a number of changes, developed by the illustrator into a logo.

Fortunately, as it turned out, the final logo was quite a lot different from the initial roughs, because soon afterwards Company A's new logo was heavily featured in a press advertising campaign and Company B immediately recognised it as being remarkably similar to the original roughs which they had been told were 'not to be used', and they were not at all pleased, to put it mildly.

In their defence the design group claimed that *they* owned the copyright because the terms of trade on their order form said so. 'Not so,' claimed the agent. 'We would never have agreed to such a thing, and anyway we sent you *our* 'acceptance of commission' form[18], which licenses the image for presentation only.'

It turned out that the front page of the design group's order form had been faxed through, which mentioned 'presentation roughs', but not the back of the form with their claim for copyright.

Why the design group behaved in this way I don't know, but if the two resulting logos had been more alike, the situation would have been disastrous for all concerned, but especially for the design group. In the end the agent and illustrator decided to let sleeping dogs lie, as the second client accepted the explanation for what had happened, and the illustrator, though he would have had a very good case for copyright infringement, was unwilling to get involved in a major copyright case.

4. An illustrator was commissioned by the Tourist Board to illustrate a number of brochure covers showing various famous buildings in the UK, among them the White Tower at the Tower of London. Since it would be impossibly expensive to visit all these sites, the illustrator used reference material from various guidebooks. His reference for the White Tower was a landscape-shaped photograph from which he produced a portrait-shaped picture, with much of the foreground clutter (queuing people, scaffolding etc) omitted, in a realistic, but slightly stylised watercolour technique. Rather surprisingly the photographer recognized his photograph and wrote to the Tourist Board demanding not just compensation but also the rendering up for destruction of all the offending brochures (they have been printed in their tens of thousands). Had the Board of Trade given in to this they could have looked to the illustrator for compensation for reprinting the brochures. Fortunately they decided to resist the claim, saying they didn't think it was a breech, because the two images were not sufficiently similar. However the photographer persisted, and the illustrator decided, although the claim for infringement could be challenged, that it was not worth risking a court case, and settled with the photographer by paying over the fee he received for the illustration – a wise decision.

7:32 Copyright infringement check–list
When in doubt, ask these questions:

1. Is the work 'infringed' itself original?

    Or is it commonplace, or itself a copy?

2. Is the infringing use a permitted act or fair dealing · ie

    Criticism, review or news reporting?

    Research or private study (not for profit)?

    An incidental use?

    Advertisement of artistic work for sale?

3. Is there evidence of copying, or could it be coincidence?

4. Does it pass the test for copyright infringement – ie

    Has a 'substantial part' of the work been taken?

    Could it be said that 'he has used the work as an inspiration; he has not copied it, but has made a new work of art of his own'?

* * *

These terms and conditions are governed by the law of

England and Wales and may not be varied except by agreement in writing.

Contracts

8

Illustration by Nancy Tolford

8 | Contracts

Every illustration commission starts with a contract, so contracts are something illustrators cannot avoid, however much they may wish they could. This section explains how the law of contract works in commissioned illustration; but it should be said right at the start that most of the complications described below can be avoided if client or illustrator use fair and reasonable standard terms of trade, and sort out any problems at the beginning of a job, rather than leaving it until after the event. The AOI Model Terms and Conditions, to be found at the beginning of this book are, we believe, a useful contribution to this end.

8:1 What is a contract?

Most people think of a contract as something written on a piece of paper, with numbered clauses, signed and dated by the parties concerned. But this is only one type of contract. In fact *any agreement – written, verbal or even partly unspoken* – is contractually binding provided it contains the following three elements:

1. An offer

2. Consideration (something in exchange – usually money)

3. Acceptance

Once these three elements are in place, the contract is created and is binding on the parties to it. Neither can alter the contract after the event without the agreement of the other.[1]

8:2 Terms at invoice/payment stage

It follows from this that the contract is made at the time of the commission or soon after. Neither side can remake the contract retrospectively. Terms of trade not sent until invoice stage (by the illustrator) or until payment (by the commissioner) have no legal force.

8:3 The importance of consideration

'Consideration' (something in exchange) is what makes the difference between a legally binding agreement and the ordinary offers we make in daily life. For instance if I offer to lend my car to a neighbour over the weekend, I am still free to change my mind at the last minute, because there is no 'consideration'. But if I offer to lend her my car for the weekend for £50, then I can't change my mind. The 'consideration' of £50, added to my offer and my neighbour's acceptance, creates a binding contract.

Consideration does not have to be money. An illustrator might agree to do work for free for, say, a printer's publicity calendar, in exchange for a few hundred printed copies (which she can then use as a mail-out), or because the printer will be sending the calendar to design companies and publishers and it will be good publicity for the illustrator. As long as the consideration is judged by a court to be of some value, it creates a binding contract.

8:4 Informal contracts

In illustration, 'informal' contracts whose terms are chiefly verbal and even 'implied' (unspoken) with a minimal written element, are common. The disadvantage of these verbal and implied contract terms is that they leave room for misunderstanding and dispute, just the sort of thing illustrators should avoid if they can.

However, informal contracts are hard to avoid entirely, so it is important for illustrators to understand how contract law works in such cases. What follows is subtle and complex, but as a general rule of thumb, contract law tries to do what is fair and reasonable. If you behave in an up-front way and make your position clear to the client in good time, you are likely to have the law on your side in any contract dispute.

8:5 The three elements

As we have already seen, once the 'three elements' are in place, the contract is binding. So how do the three elements – offer, consideration and acceptance – work out in practice? Here are two examples:

1. Rodney Lunch, art editor of *Guzzler* magazine, phones an illustrator wanting a half-page colour illustration; roughs in a week, artwork two days later. That's the *offer*.

   'What's the fee?' asks the illustrator. 'Can't pay more than £250,' says Rodney. That's the *consideration*.

   'OK,' says the illustrator. That's the acceptance.

   The three elements are in place and the contract is created and is binding.

2. Supposing the illustrator were a bit better at bargaining, and when Rodney says the fee is £250, the illustrator says, 'Can't you squeeze a bit more out of the budget? I normally reckon to get £350 for a half-page.' In this case Rodney has made an offer with consideration, but instead of accepting, the illustrator has made a *counter-offer*.

   'I can go up to £300,' says Rodney. This is a *counter-counter-offer*.

   If the illustrator agrees, there is acceptance, the three elements are in place, and the contract is created.

1. Though many social and family arrangements do not amount to contracts, even when there is consideration, if the court thinks they were not intended to be legally binding. (In the unlikely event that you need to know more about this, it can be found under 'Social and Domestic Arrangements' in *The Law of Contract* by G. H. Treitel, a standard reference work on contract law.)

8:6 Standard of proof

At this point you may be thinking 'How can anyone prove that something has been agreed in a telephone call if it's not written down on a piece of paper?' The answer is that in civil law (the law which deals with non-criminal matters like contract disputes) the standard of proof required is quite different from proof in criminal law. In criminal law the prosecution must prove their case 'beyond reasonable doubt' – a very high standard of proof. In civil law all that is required is to prove something 'on the balance of probability', which is a lot easier. That is why O. J. Simpson was found not guilty of murdering his wife by a criminal court, but liable for compensation in relationship to the same events, in a case brought by his wife's family, in a civil court.

8:7 Evidence

Returning to Rodney Lunch and *Guzzler* magazine for the moment, let's suppose that the next thing that happens is that Rodney faxes a copy of the article to the illustrator on which he has written 'Cheers – Rodney'. When the illustrator gets it, she scribbles on it the fee that has been agreed, and dates for rough and artwork. We now have a contract that was arrived at verbally, and is evidenced not just by the recollection of Rodney and the illustrator, but also by Rodney's fax and the illustrator's own note about the fee and the delivery dates. This may sound pretty flimsy, but it's likely to be good enough for a court applying the 'balance of probability' standard of proof. A written note of a verbal agreement, made at the time (known as a 'contemporaneous note'), is usually accepted by courts as good evidence.

8:8 Contracts: implied terms[2]

The idea of an implied or 'unspoken' term of a contract may seem puzzling at first. In fact such 'implied terms' are often found in informal contracts. They cannot contradict an agreed (or 'express') term, but they can add to what has been agreed to fill in any gaps. The easiest way to see how implied terms work is to look at some specific instances.

8:9 'Of the same mind'

A term of a contract may be implied because both parties agree about something when they make the contract, even though they don't mention it. In legal jargon they are said to be 'ad idem' – or, in English – 'of the same mind'. Another way of thinking about this is 'too obvious to mention' or 'it goes without saying'.

To go back to Rodney Lunch and *Guzzler* magazine, suppose that he rings the illustrator, offers the work and the illustrator accepts; but neither of them thinks to mention the fee. The illustrator does the work, and needs to send an invoice. What is the contract between the two? Is there any contract? After all, there was no fee agreed so there seems to have been no consideration.

Though courts will sometimes refuse to uphold a contract if the amount of the consideration is unspecified, in a case like this it would probably say that both sides clearly intended there would be a fee and were therefore 'of the same mind' on the issue, so it would be reasonable to imply that term into the contract and uphold it. The court would then have to look to see if it could decide what the fee should be. It might do this on a 'quantum meruit' basis (Latin for 'how much is it worth?') in which case expert evidence on typical magazine fees might be heard to decide what fee was reasonable. Or the court might use another type of implied term to decide the fee, a term implied by conduct.

8:10 Conduct

A term can be implied by the conduct of one or other of the parties. In the case of our Rodney Lunch saga, the court might decide that the illustrator, by not enquiring what the fee was before she did the artwork, had implied *by her conduct* that she was willing to accept, whatever the magazine's usual fee was, and settle the amount on that basis.

In contract law it is usually the case (because of the notion of implication by conduct) that 'silence implies acceptance'. For instance, if a client offers me a job that I am eager to do, but the contract they send with the offer is horrendous (a demand for assignment of copyright, say) and says I must sign the contract and return it to the client, I might decide to do the job but not to return the signed contract, hoping they won't notice. I haven't signed the contract, so I haven't agreed to their horrible terms, right?

Sadly, I would be wrong. By doing the job without making any explicit objection to their contract terms, the law would say that I have accepted their offer – because I have implied acceptance by my silence and by carrying out the work– by doing the job without objecting to the terms.[3]

This is the principle which underlies the 'Battle of the Forms' (see 8:15).

8:11 Business efficacy

Suppose that Rodney Lunch and the illustrator agreed on the fee for the job at the time of the commission, but said nothing about the licence for reproduction that *Guzzler* magazine would have. After the illustrator has delivered the artwork and sent in her invoice, a cheque from *Guzzler* arrives in the post. On the back of the cheque is printed 'I hereby assign complete copyright and ownership of the artwork to *Guzzler* Magazine Ltd' and an accompanying letter tells the illustrator that the cheque cannot be cleared unless she signs this. Does she have to?

No, because it was not part of the original contract that she made at the time of the commission, even by implication. She and Rodney were not 'of the same mind' about this, nor could she have signalled her acceptance of *Guzzler's* terms by silence, since the terms were never put to her.

So what licence has transferred? In answering this question the law would try to look at what is reasonable in all the circumstances. There has been an agreement to transfer rights, but the extent of the rights was never specified; what rights would it be necessary to transfer to 'give business efficacy' to the contract (in other words to make the bargain work from a business point of view)? Clearly a transfer of copyright is much more than *Guzzler* needs to illustrate an article in its magazine. A court would probably find that 'one use', exclusive to it for a reasonable period, is what the magazine needs. As for ownership of the artwork, a purchaser of a reproduction right does not thereby get to own the artwork, and there is no reason of business efficacy why *Guzzler* should be entitled to own it.

8:12 Previous course of trading

Suppose that *Guzzler* has been commissioning our illustrator over the past two years to do a monthly illustration for their popular 'Bulimics Anonymous' column, each time sending her an outrageous contract at the time of the commission which demands the complete copyright and ownership of artwork. Our illustrator, who feels she can't afford to turn down regular work, has foolishly agreed to this in the past, and returned the magazine's contract duly signed.

2. A 'term' of a contract is a bit of the contract dealing with a specific issue – for instance it may be a term of the contract that the illustrator should be credited.

3. So, although I will not yet have assigned my copyright (because it is a principle of law that copyright cannot be assigned except in writing), I *will* have agreed that I will assign my copyright, and the client can then make me put it in writing by demanding 'specific performance of the contract'. This can be a trap for the unwary.

Then one month the commission comes, but without its nasty contract because for once Guzzler magazine has forgotten to send it. After she has done the artwork, *Guzzler* realise their mistake and send her the contract. Must she sign it, or can she say; 'No this was not part of our original agreement?'

A court may well decide that even though this time the contract had not been sent, because the two had worked on the same basis over a long period in the past (previous course of trading), the illustrator knew what *Guzzler's* terms were and *Guzzler* was entitled to rely on the assumption that unless otherwise stated by either side, the terms would be the same as before.

8:13 Trade practice

A trade practice or custom can create a term of a contract if it is 'reasonable and prevalent in the trade'. By this test, trade customs such as the illustrator being credited for editorial work but not for advertising work would be capable of implying a term into a contract, or even (though this may not be prevalent enough) the commonly used 50% rejection fee[4].

8:14 Written agreements

All the complications and uncertainties of informal agreements can be done away with if one side or the other uses a properly drafted written contract which deals with all the issues relevant to the commission. That will give certainty about exactly what has been agreed, as well as reliable proof.

The more work a job entails, the more important it is to have a written contract. If a one-off magazine job goes horribly wrong, and the illustrator ends up unpaid, it's not the end of the world. If the same thing happens with a major project that has taken several months, a properly drafted fair contract is an important protection for both sides.

The trouble is that if the contract comes from the commissioner, the illustrator may find that the terms are quite disadvantageous – sometimes downright dreadful. She then has the choice of trying to negotiate changes to the client's contract or, if the client's contract is hopeless unsuitable, she may decide to send a contract of her own.

This gives rise to what is called 'The Battle of the Forms'.

8:15 The Battle of the Forms

What happens if both sides present different terms and conditions to each other? Suppose, for instance, Guzzler Magazine sends the illustrator an order spelling out their demands for copyright assignment and artwork ownership; and instead of signing and returning it, the illustrator sends her own 'acceptance of commission' form with her own terms and conditions on it. Which of the two sets of terms and conditions form the contract?

The general rule is that *the last set of terms wins* (ie in this case the illustrator has said, 'Yes, I accept the commission, but on my terms' – in effect a counter-offer – and the client's conduct in proceeding with the commission without objection implies consent). But there may be uncertainties. For instance, if the illustrator's 'acceptance' terms are sent very late in the day, a court may think that the client had no time to find another illustrator, and decide they are not valid. In general, though, the rule 'last one wins' can be relied on.

4. See 'Rejection and Cancellation fees' (Appendix B).

5. If you need to know what this is and how to set it up, consult a geek.

6. This contrasts with copyright law, where an illustrator may take an action against anyone involved in a breach of copyright, even if they are unaware of it – just one of the reasons why illustrators should hang on to their copyrights.

7. Said by Sir Walter Raleigh's son, when hitting the person next to him at table. He was annoyed with his father, who was sitting at the same table some places away. The situation is complicated by the recent Contracts (Rights of Third Parties) Act 1999, which makes it possible for people who are not parties to a contract to sue someone who is, but only if the former benefit under the contract. Best not to rely on it as a general rule of thumb.

8. 'Reasonable' depends on the circumstances. Clearly if the a/d goes back on his word so late in the day that it's impossible for me to get the work done in time, that's not reasonable.

8:16 Proof of sending

If the illustrator is going to send her own terms of trade she will have to be able to prove, on the balance of probability, that the terms were in fact sent. The law says that once a letter is posted to the correct address, it is assumed to be delivered and to have been received by the other party, even if it gets lost in the post. This is unfair, but there seems to be no satisfactory way of resolving the issue, so contract law has made this completely arbitrary rule as a matter of 'public policy'.

The illustrator will still need to show that the letter has actually been posted. A copy of the letter, dated, might very well do. A copy of the contract with a 'contemporaneous note' saying when it was sent would be better. Better still would be a fax, because there will be supporting evidence from the fax record that a document had actually gone to that number on the date in question. Also good is an email, since a permanent record of this remains (though there's no proof it actually got through, so an 'answerback' facility would be ideal).[5]

8:17 Changing your mind

Suppose an illustrator accepts a commission, then regrets it and wants to change her mind. In theory the commissioner could insist on her doing the job, because her agreement is binding provided the 'three elements' are in place. In practice no commissioner is likely to want to use an unwilling illustrator, and provided there is time to find someone else, is likely to release her from the contract. But the commissioner doesn't have to.

8:18 'Privity' of contract

Contracts are usually valid only against the parties who agreed to them.[6] In a recent case an illustrator was commissioned by a publisher to illustrate a book, and in the course of publication the original artwork was lost. The illustrator demanded compensation for the loss from the publisher, but the publisher said 'It's not my fault. You must get your compensation from the printers. They're the ones who lost it.'

In fact the publisher was wrong. The illustrator has no contract with the printer, so cannot get compensation from him. The illustrator *does* have a contract with the publisher, so must sue the publisher. In turn the publisher, who has got a contract with the printer, can sue the printer. The printer may blame the plate-maker, in which case the printer must sue the plate-maker; and so on down the line until it gets to the person who actually lost the artwork. This is a legal version of 'Box about, 'Twill come to my father anon.'[7]

8:19 Variations in contracts

It often happens that a contract is agreed and then one party or the other wants to change it. Typically the illustrator might want an extra day to finish the work, or the client may want to use the image for additional purposes.

The general rule is that if the variation benefits only one party (and not the other) then it is not legally binding unless there is some extra 'consideration' given in exchange to the party who does not benefit.

For instance if I am due to deliver some artwork on Friday, but the art director says I can have until Monday so that I can attend my child's school play, there is no benefit to the art director. He can still go back on his word and insist on delivery by Friday – provided he gives me reasonable notice.[8]

In the other common example, where a client asks for extra reproduction rights to those originally agreed, the same principal applies. If the client wants to make the variation binding, it has to give some consideration – typically an extra amount of money. Otherwise the illustrator can change her mind, provided she gives reasonable notice.

To add further complication, a principle of law known as 'estoppel' may operate here. Estoppel[9] prevents someone going back on their word if the other party has relied on it. Thus if, on the basis that I have until Monday to finish my artwork, I take on another job for delivery by Friday (which I am also then contractually bound to do), the first art director may be *estopped* (think 'stopped') from insisting on his original Friday delivery date, because I have relied on his word to take on an extra job. Similarly, if I agree to an extension of the reproduction rights in my image beyond the original agreement, and on the basis of this the commissioner makes a binding agreement for the job to his client, I may be estopped from going back on my word, even though there's no consideration and I've given reasonable notice, because the commissioner has relied on my variation of the contract.

8:20 Vagueness or ambiguity in contracts

Clients' written contracts can sometimes be vague, or even self-contradictory, especially if they have taken a standard contract and added a bit of amateurish tweaking themselves. I once came across a contract which said in one clause that the illustrator granted certain limited reproduction rights, and in another that the illustrator assigned the whole copyright.

A contract may be so vague that the law declares it void, but courts will generally try to avoid this, and will resolve the vagueness either by custom, or test of reasonableness or, if the phrase in question is meaningless, by ignoring it.

In the case of ambiguous or contradictory terms the law will generally interpret these *against* the interest of the party that drew up the contract.

8:21 Incomplete contracts

We have seen (above: 'What is a contract?') that once the elements of *offer, acceptance* and *consideration* are in place, a contract is made. At this stage there may be several details of the contract that have not yet been agreed. The law will still greatly prefer to uphold the incomplete contract if it can, and if necessary decide the parts that have not been agreed by applying a test of 'reasonableness'. Even if there is no agreement about the price to be paid, provided there is an express or implied agreement that there will be an unspecified sum paid, the contract will be upheld, and if necessary the price set on a test of 'reasonableness'.

If an illustrator wants to make a quote without binding herself until the full details of the contract have been worked out, then the quote should be made headed, 'subject to contract'.

8:22 'Personal' contracts

Generally speaking if a company is taken over by another company, the new owners 'inherit' all the contractual benefits and obligations from the business they have bought. The contracts are said to be 'assigned' to the new owners.

However, there is an exception to this if the contract involves 'personal services', in which one party relies on the talents or qualities of a particular person.

9. From the Old French *Estoupail* meaning a stopper or plug. It's a left-over from the Norman French that was used in the courts in medieval times.

10. The usual wording to allow assignment is that the contract is with 'The XYZ Co Ltd, their assigns or successors in business'. This wording is common in publishing contracts, but is usually limited by a standard 'protection clause'. See 10:48.

11. Or, in legal language, 'nullified' or 'voided'.

Thus an illustrator cannot usually assign the contract for an illustration job to another illustrator, because the commissioner relies on the skills of the particular illustrator it has chosen; and a publisher cannot assign the benefit of an author's contract to another publisher unless the agreement specifically says that they can.[10]

In a recent case an illustrator had a (very bad) agreement with her agent which stipulated, among other things, that an image once submitted to the agent for exploitation, remained to be exploited exclusively by that agent indefinitely, even after the illustrator had left the agency.

The agency then went bankrupt. In normal circumstances a bankrupt business would, if possible, be sold on by the receiver, and the new owner would 'inherit' the benefit of all those images which the agency had the sole right to exploit. However, the illustrator was able to argue that her contract with the agency was 'personal', and so the benefit of her contract with the agency could not be assigned to anyone else. She was freed from her agreement (since the original company had gone bust and no longer existed) and could place her images elsewhere.

8:23 Remedies for breach of contract

There are two basic remedies if one party fails to do what they have agreed to, 'specific performance' and 'damages'. A claim for specific performance asks the court to order the defendant to do what it has contracted to do. For instance, an illustrator might claim for specific performance in order to get her artwork returned by her client.

An alternative is to ask for damages (money). In deciding the amount of money to award, the court will try to put the claimant in the position she would have been in if the defendant had performed the contract properly. For instance if a claimant asks for her artwork back, or (if the artwork is lost) damages instead (damages in lieu), the court, in judging the amount of damages, will look at the value of the artwork and any money the claimant may have lost because she did not have the artwork (for example if she could show that she had lost a valuable commission because she did not have the artwork – improbable but possible).

Courts may sometimes award damages for fairly speculative matters, such as 'loss of valuable publicity and enhancement of reputation' resulting from the non-publication of something the defendant undertook to publish. These, however, are hard to quantify and rarely awarded.

In rare instances, when particularly outraged at the conduct of the offending party, the court may award additional damages for the 'flagrancy' of the defendant's acts.

8:24 Invalid contracts

Although the law prefers wherever possible to uphold apparent contracts, there are circumstances where a contract may be declared invalid.[11] They are:

8:25 Illegality

If the contract is to do something illegal, for instance if an illustrator and commissioner knowingly agree to copy someone else's image in breach of copyright. But if one or both parties are unaware that the act is illegal, the situation is more complicated.

If one party knows and the other doesn't, the one who knows may not be able to claim under the contract. Suppose a client knowingly commissions an illustrator to copy someone else's work, and halfway through the job the illustrator discovers what's going on and refuses to finish it. In that situation the illustrator (who didn't know) could claim, under the contract, payment for the work she had already done; but the client (who *did* know it was illegal) could not claim under the contract against the illustrator (for instance to complete the work, or for damages for non-completion). If neither party knows of the illegality, then the contract is legal.

8:26 Mistake

Where there is a fundamental mistake; because they intended to contract about different things (for instance if, as happened in a real case, a client says it 'wants to own the artwork', meaning it wants to be able to reproduce the artwork in any way it likes, but the illustrator quotes on the basis that it wants merely to own the physical artwork and have a limited licence); or because they are mistaken about the subject matter (for instance if an artist is commissioned to paint a portrait, but unknown to both parties the subject of the portrait is dead); or because the contract is physically or legally impossible to carry out; or because of a mistake as to the quality of something (for instance if something is wrongly described at auction).

8:27 Duress

If there is duress, meaning threats to the person, or to property.[12] It has been proposed that this should be extended to asking 'whether or not the agreement in question is to be regarded as having been concluded voluntarily'. In any event it seems clear that there must be actual or threatened wrongful conduct and 'mere commercial pressure' is not enough to invalidate a contract, which is a shame.

8:28 Inequality of bargaining power

Inequality of bargaining power is such a feature of some illustration commissions that I mention here a principle propounded by Lord Denning[13], though it seems not yet to have gained general acceptance. 'The English law gives relief to one who, *without independent advice*[14], enters into a contract upon terms which are very unfair...when his bargaining power is grievously impaired by reason of his own needs or desires, or by his own ignorance or infirmity, *coupled with* undue influence brought to bear on him by or for the benefit of another.'

This principle may be worth a try, even though it is fairly unlikely that a court will accept it in most cases. There has been quite a lot of success with this principle in the music industry in cases like long-term agreements with agents foolishly entered into, from which it would appear to be more relevant to long-term contracts. But beware, it is still the case that a person is bound by the terms of a written contract even though she has not read them.

8:29 Frustration

A contract is said to be 'frustrated' if something which both parties regard as necessary to the performance of the contract no longer exists. For instance, if a right-handed illustrator breaks her right arm or if an illustrator is commissioned to make drawings of an event which is subsequently cancelled. In either case the contract would be void.

8:30 Vague or incomplete

Contracts can sometimes be void because they are too vague or incomplete. Generally though the law will try to uphold contracts, and will interpret missing or vague terms as best it can, especially if it appears that both parties intended to contract at the time, or if the incomplete contract has already been performed by one of the parties.

8:31 Contract analysis checklist

Use this checklist to help analyse a contract situation

1. Who are the parties to the contract? (who is it between).

2. Is there a chain of contracts? If so, which person in the chain is the contract with? Might the Contracts (Third Party) Act apply?/ (see 8:18f).

3. What was the offer, what was the consideration? Was there a counter-offer?

4. When was the offer/counter offer (with consideration) accepted? (At this point the contract was created).

5. At the time of the creation of the contract –

   What terms had been agreed in writing? (including contemporaneous notes).

   What terms had been agreed verbally?

   What terms might have been implied?

6. Were there any mutually agreed variations in the contract before the contract was performed (eg before delivery of the artwork)?

7. Was the contract performed satisfactorily?

8. Was there anything which might make the contract invalid?

8:32 Clients' contracts checklist

A few basic points to look out for

1. Appropriate licence or rights grab?

2. Artwork ownership?

3. Fee?

4. Delivery date realistic?

5. Credits?

6. Warranties (any use of 'alleged' breach?)

7. Is client supplying picture reference? (Is it copyright cleared?)

8. Governing law? (UK is best).

Especially for long / high price jobs

1. Cancellation fee.

2. Rejection fee.

12. Fortunately a very rare situation for an illustrator to find herself in, but by coincidence I am dealing with a case of alleged threats as I write, so I have included it.

13. Lloyd's Bank v Bundy [1975] QB 326; ante p 310

14. The italics in this quote are my own. The principle is really quite restricted. In a recent case in which I was trying to get back rights from the OUP which they should never have acquired, the fact that the illustrator had had independent advice on the original contract counted against her.

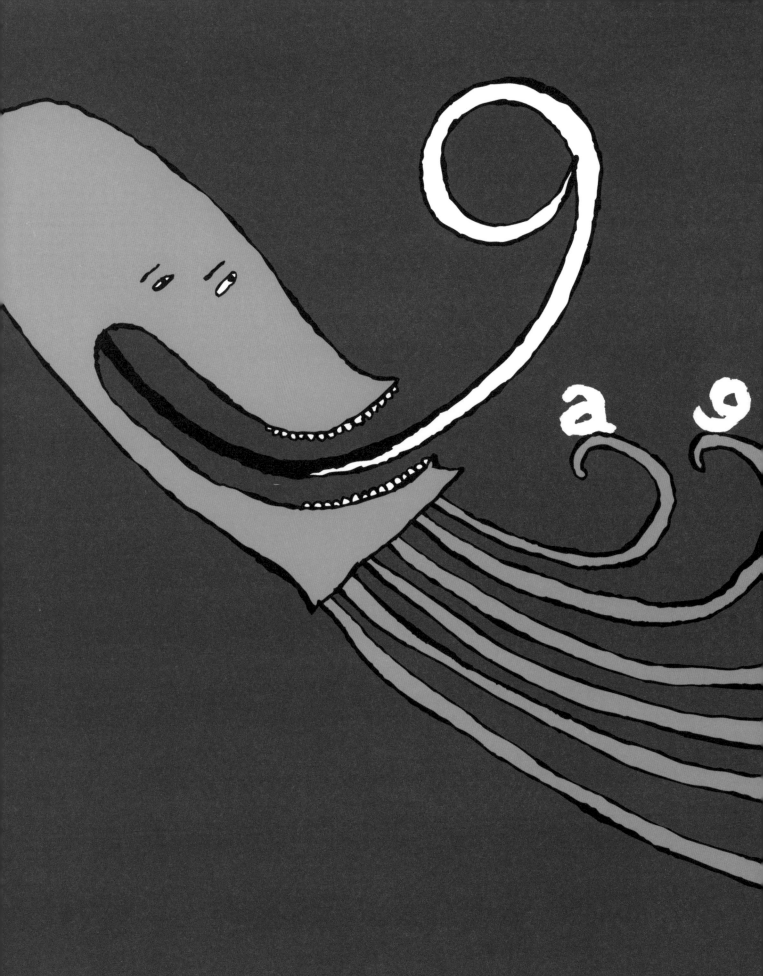

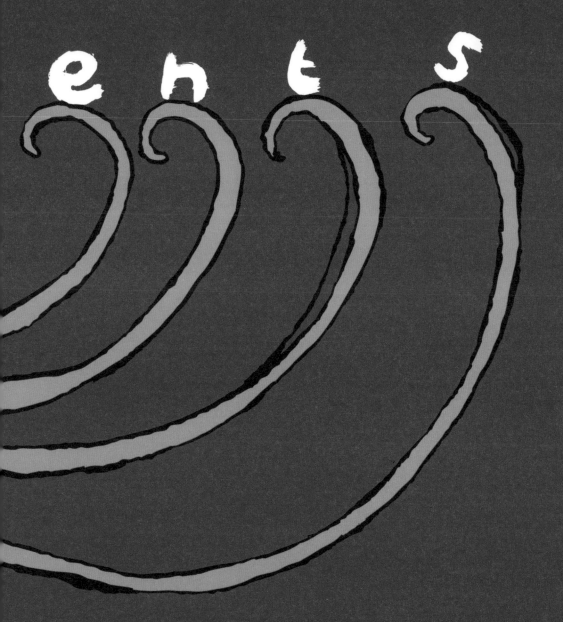

9 Agents

Illustrator agencies vary a lot – in the character of the people who run them, in the type of work they represent, in the nature of the businesses themselves. A good relationship with an agent can be very useful to an illustrator, but finding the right agent is not always easy. Until someone publishes a guide to the different agents, word of mouth and trial and error are all illustrators have to guide them. All the more important, then, to be clear about the agreement between illustrator and agent right from the beginning, so that each party knows what they are letting themselves in for.

9:1 The legal meaning of 'agent'

The word 'agent' has a precise legal meaning. Some so-called 'agents' are not legally agents at all. On the other hand lots of people *are* legally agents, though they may not be aware of it; for instance all employees are *agents* of their employers. If a staff member of the Association of Illustrators books a hall for an AOI meeting, the staff member will not be personally liable for the booking fee. The AOI will be liable for the fee, because the staff member, acting as an agent of the AOI, has created a contract between the owners of the hall and the AOI.

The person or entity on whose behalf the agent acts is called the agent's *principal*. The *principal* employs the *agent*, and the agency takes instructions and makes agreements not on its own behalf, but on behalf of its principal.

In illustration the relationship between artist and agent is not quite as simple as that between employer and employee. Though the artist is the principal – and therefore the boss – the agency will also represent other artists, each with their own interests. The relationship is more like that between a solicitor or accountant and his/her client.

The artist *is* the boss is some respects. It's very important, for instance, that the artist should know what licences are being granted on his/her behalf, what invoices are being sent out and should be consulted and have the last word on things like price, deadline and so forth, because when an agency accepts a commission on behalf of one of its artists, it creates a contract not between the agency and the client, but between the artist and the client.

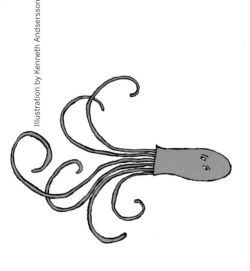

Illustration by Kenneth Andsersson

In other respects the relationship is much more equal. The agent may want to make conditions, such as that every artist is expected to do a certain minimum of promotion each year. I discuss some of these issues below.

9:2 What agents do for illustrators

Agents will not magically get work for illustrators. On the whole work follows the illustrator, not the agent. However the agent should:

- Enhance the illustrator's earnings, especially if the illustrator has not been promoting him/herself effectively.

- Give the illustrator access to 'agent only' annuals.

- Give the illustrator access to those advertising art buyers who prefer to source their illustration through an agent.

- Give the illustrator access to certain types of promotion which an individual artist would find hard to organise, such as:
  Special agency promotion packs.
  Promotion trips abroad.
  Joint promotion with others – eg printers and designers.

- Make regular visits with the portfolio to clients.

- Keep your portfolio updated and fresh.

- Negotiate for you – especially important with advertising and design jobs, where fees are highly negotiable and copyright issues are sometimes a problem.

- Do all your invoicing and other paperwork.

- Do your proof and artwork chasing.

- Act as a buffer between you and the client when necessary.

- Some agencies have reciprocal arrangements with agencies in other countries.

9:3 Agreements with agents

Few agents have a formal written contract, taking the view that the relationship either works or it doesn't, and a contract won't help. As a matter of fact all the formal, written agent's contracts I have seen have been drawn up in a very one-sided way against the interests of the illustrator. So if an illustrator gets such an agreement, he/she should make sure it is checked.

It is often not realised that even if no written agreement exists between agent and illustrator there is still a contract between them, though its terms are largely implied and uncertain unless and until they are tested in court.

To avoid this uncertainty, if there is no formal contract there ought at least to be some sort of written checklist of what the agency is offering to do, and what it expects from the illustrator. Otherwise the illustrator may have an unrealistic idea of what the agency will deliver, which if it is not fulfilled, can lead to ill-feeling and the sort of mutual suspicion that sometimes spoils an illustrator/agent relationship.

The following is a checklist of the issues that should be clarified between illustrator and agent, and ideally confirmed in writing by one side or the other. Confirmation in an informal letter will suffice.

9:4 Area and market

Both sides should be clear about what geographical area is to be covered (UK, Europe, USA, etc) and what type of work (advertising, design group, editorial, etc). Many agents concentrate on the higher paid areas – advertising and design group – and some are content to let the illustrator deal with editorial work him/herself. Some agencies may also be prepared to let the illustrator handle certain clients with whom he/she has built up a close relationship in the past, or over which a previous agent has rights for a limited period (though on the whole agents dislike such agreements).

Book publishing, especially where royalties are concerned, is an area which illustrators should consider retaining. Unless the agency specialises in this field, it may not be competent to deal with publishing contracts, and the normal illustrator's agency commission compares badly with that of literary agents and may make many projects financially unattractive in this often poorly paid field. (See Section 10: Royalty Agreements).

When illustrators' agents do deal with a book illustration commission, an appropriate arrangement may be for the agency to take a commission on the advance on royalties, but not on further earnings from the book, or to take a reduced commission on future earnings.

9:5 Who else does the agency represent?

This is not something that needs to be agreed, but is something an illustrator should find out to get some idea of what the agency is about.

Conventional wisdom used to be that about 7·8 illustrators per member of staff is the most that an agency can handle well, and that the staff/illustrator ratio should not be much lower than that (counting all staff, not just representatives); but that was in the 80s, when illustration was booming, and these days few agencies can afford to be so generously staffed. It's unrealistic these days. However a very large number of artists and few staff may be an indication that the agency is not bringing in a lot of work for many of their artists.

9:6 How much work?

Illustrator and agency should be clear about whether the aim is to keep the illustrator in full employment – or conversely, in the case of a book/editorial illustrator who wants to handle a lot of work him/herself, how much work the agency expects the illustrator to do through it to be financially viable from the agency's point of view.

9:7 Commission

Basic commissions currently range from 25 to 30%, and many agencies charge different commissions for different markets · 20% for editorial, 30% for advertising and design group, 40% for work outside the UK, for instance.

9:8 Promotion expenses

It should be made clear what regular promotions the agency does which the artist is expected to participate in and how much each side will contribute to promotion expenses. A common arrangement is that the agent contributes the same percentage as their basic commission rate, and the artist pays the rest. Agencies are often willing to deduct the illustrator's share from future earnings if necessary.

Other expenses such as messenger services (where necessary) are normally paid for by the agency, though the illustrator is responsible for getting the artwork to the agent. Broadband has made this something of a non-issue.

Any other items which the agency charges for (eg portfolios) should be defined.

9:9 Terms and conditions

The illustrator should have a copy of the standard terms and conditions under which the agency trades, and know what the agency's policy is about accepting clients' terms and conditions. For instance, does the agency normally consult the illustrator before accepting terms and conditions other than their own? Or only if the client's terms are exceptionally onerous?

Policy about parting with copyright and artwork ownership are particularly important areas which both sides should be clear about. Almost all agencies are careful not to part with copyright, but some are less concerned about artwork ownership.

The best agencies chase artwork and proofs regularly and keep their illustrators informed of any problems.

So far as the return of artwork is concerned, the agency should make sure ownership is part of their terms and conditions, and should make reasonable efforts to get artwork back. It is not reasonable to expect them to guarantee its return, however, or to be financially accountable for its loss. It can be very difficult and time-consuming to get artwork back from some clients and, especially if the illustration is not especially valued by the artist, may not be worth pursuing.

9:10 Invoicing

Agencies vary in their methods of financial accounting.

It is important to know whether an agency is invoicing the client on its own behalf, or on the illustrator's behalf.

If it is invoicing on its own behalf it will quote its own VAT number (and may require the illustrator to invoice the agency).

If it is invoicing on the illustrator's behalf it will quote the illustrator's VAT number, or will not charge VAT if the illustrator is not registered.

The difference can be important should the agency go bankrupt. If the agency invoices on its own behalf, then all outstanding invoices will, when paid, belong to the agency. The illustrator will be an unsecured creditor, and may not see his/her share.

But if the agency invoices on the illustrator's behalf, then although the money still passes through the agency account, the agency will only be entitled to its commission and the illustrator should be protected.

Ideally it should be made clear in writing that funds collected are held in trust for the illustrator. This, however, seldom happens.

There is one advantage to the illustrator if the agency invoices on its own behalf. This is that the agency's commission does not form part of the illustrator's turnover, and the illustrator may therefore be able to keep below the ceiling at which it becomes compulsory to register for VAT. In practice, though, since the agency has to charge VAT on its commission, the illustrator will be better off registering for VAT, even if he/she is below the compulsory ceiling, so that the VAT on commission can be reclaimed.

There are no obvious disadvantages to the agency if it invoices in the illustrator's name.

9:11 Accounting to the illustrator

The agency should say how and when they pay the illustrator. Best practice is for the agency to make a monthly return to the illustrator with copies of all invoices sent and payment for all invoices paid in the preceding month.

Illustrators should always have the right to inspect the agency accounts, and illustrators would be well advised to have this, at least, confirmed in writing. It is a sad fact that agencies occasionally go bankrupt, sometimes owing individual illustrators many thousands of pounds, so this is an essential protection for the illustrator who suspects that something may be going wrong. Moreover, it is standard practice whenever one person holds money on behalf of another, that the holder should grant this right; (for instance it forms a part of every standard royalty contract).

If an agency wishes to protect confidentiality about the affairs of other illustrators there is nothing to stop it stipulating that inspection should be carried out by a qualified accountant who undertakes to disclose only what is relevant to the illustrator concerned.

Few clients in advertising and design groups pay promptly, but an illustrator who finds a large number of invoices still unpaid after four or five months may have cause for concern. A recent survey of 50 sequential jobs in one illustrator's largely design/advertising practice showed that 12% of clients paid in one month, 12% in two months, 28% in three months, 34% in four months, 6% in five months, 4% in six months, and 4% in seven months – the longest period any invoice remained outstanding, though longer periods have been known in other cases.

9:12 Agency liability

Ideally agents should be insured against loss of artwork and liability to their illustrators resulting from negligence (though as far as I know few are). However, loss of artwork insurance especially can be very hard to get, involve a lot of bureaucracy, and many agents don't have it.

9:13 Parting company

This is one of the most contentious areas in the agent/illustrator relationship, and arrangements for terminating the agreement should be clear in advance.

Agents get annoyed if, having promoted an illustrator's career and made him/her successful, the illustrator then says, 'Thanks, but I'm leaving. Now that I'm successful, I don't need to pay your commission.' There is no perfect solution to this problem. An arrangement recommended by the US Graphic Arts Guild is that after termination the agency is entitled to commission on any work received from clients originally obtained by the agency, for a period of three months if the illustrator was with the agency for six months or less, plus one month for every additional six months the illustrator was with the agency, up to a maximum of six months.

It's a good idea to agree about this in writing at the start of the relationship.

1. For a listing of literary agents, consult the Writers and Artists Yearbook.

2. DACS
33 Gt Sutton St
London EC1V 0DX
tel: 020 7336 8811
(www.dacs.org.uk)

Other types of agencies

9:14 Literary agents

Literary agents are ideal for illustrators who specialise in children's books. They charge less than mainstream agents – typically 10-15% for UK and 15-20% for overseas. They specialise in the publishing field, and will also deal with negotiating royalty contracts for you, something which most mainstream illustrators' agents are not qualified to do. Anyone who does a significant amount of book work should consider using a literary agent for representation in this area.

Not all agents deal with children's books, and of those who do, not all are prepared to take on illustrators.[1]

9:15 Collecting societies

Collecting societies deal with licences which individual creators and their agents cannot handle themselves. The collecting society for the visual arts in the UK is The Design and Artists Copyright Society (DACS)[2] and it handles money for photocopying, cable re-transmission on TV, and slide collections, distributing money through its annual 'Payback' campaign. Any illustrator who has had work published in books or magazines should make a claim for 'Payback' money.

DACS also administers Resale Right, which pays a proportion of the price of a work of art when it is sold on for 1,000 Euros or more by an art market professional, and mostly affects fine artists.

9:16 Card and gift agencies

There are a few agencies specialising in the greetings card and giftware markets, mostly dealing with existing imagery which they licence. They nearly all have written contracts, and I have yet to see one from the UK that I would be willing to sign. Avoid any contract which says that once you place an image with the agent it stays with them forever.

However in the USA these types of agents seem to have much more artist-friendly contracts, and since that's where the biggest market is, it's worth looking for a USA agent if this is your field.

The standard commission for this sort of agency is 50%.

9:17 Stock agencies

Photographers have lodged their images with image libraries (so-called 'stock' photographs) for years, but stock agencies for illustration are more recent and a lot more controversial. The UK Association of Illustrators, as well as the USA Society of Illustrators and Graphic Arts Guild, are against stock, on the grounds that it sells illustration cheap and brings down fees for first time commissions. Others take the view that stock is here to stay, so we might as well join in.

Some stock agencies expect the illustrator to pay for space in their catalogues, others do not, and some are wholly web-based. Artists should think hard before paying for space in an agency's catalogue. Bear in mind, too, that the largest market for stock is the USA, so it makes little sense to be with a Europe based sub-agency if that means that the US *and* the local agency both take a commission. Better be with a US-based agent.

The Illustrator's Guide to Law and Business Practice

Most agents of this sort take a commission of 50%, though the web-based ones are more likely to charge an annual fee rather than take a commission. There are some 'creator friendly' stock libraries, run by agencies or by , for instance, the US i-spot.

9:18 Be nice to your agent

Some illustrators think agents are on a par with estate agents, suspect that agents make a fortune out of artists and regard them as at best a necessary evil. That is not my experience. There are a few dodgy agents about, but for the most part they work hard for their money. Running an illustration agency is not a path to an easy fortune.

A very successful cartoonist I know once acted as an agent for a short while and reports that it was the most unpleasant experience of his life, largely because a few of the illustrators behaved so appallingly. Another ex-agent of my acquaintance tells how he spent months wooing a particular client and at last got a substantial job for one of his artists. Come deadline day the artist concerned confessed that she had not done the job, couldn't cope with it and had been too embarrassed to say anything before. Needless to say the whole agency was affected by this, and months of schmoozing wasted.

So here are a few rules for having a good relationship with your agent:

1. In the first place choose an agent you get on with and are happy with. Remember if one agency is interested in your work, it's likely others will be.

2. If you have queries, or things you are dissatisfied with, be upfront about them. Don't seethe in silence.

3. Keep your agent informed: if you are going away on holiday, or even away from the studio for a day, remember to let the agency know.

4. Never, *ever*, under any circumstances go behind your agent's back. If you have agreed they will handle all advertising work, don't accept a nice job on the side to avoid agent's commission. Firstly it's dishonest, and secondly the agent will almost certainly find out and never trust you again.

AGREEMENTS

Illustration by Andy Smith

10 | **Royalty Agreements**

Royalty agreements are nearly always longer and more complicated than ordinary 'one off' illustration contracts because they are usually designed to last for the whole period of copyright (seventy years after the author/illustrator's death) and have to take account of what may happen during that time. It is common, and perfectly acceptable, to have detailed negotiations over royalty contracts. This section deals mostly with children's book publishing, but the principles described in it will be found helpful in considering any type of royalty agreement.

10:1 What are royalty agreements?

When an illustrator signs a royalty contract with a publisher, he/she is entering into a relationship in which the illustrator contributes creative skill and expertise, and in return the publisher puts up the money and contributes his expertise in manufacturing, marketing and distributing. The publisher hopes to make a profit selling the books and other rights, and passes on to the author/illustrator a share of the proceeds in the form of *royalties*.

The agreement between illustrator and publisher lasts usually (though not always)[1] until the end of the copyright period – more than 100 years if the illustrator is young and long-lived – and therefore has to take into account all sorts of eventualities; so royalty agreements tend to be long and complicated. Fortunately, over the years their form has become largely standardized, which makes life easier. A variety of standard publishing contracts with detailed notes can be found in *Publishing Agreements* by Charles Clarke (Allen and Unwin) and anyone who is likely to be working in the book field should get hold of a copy and look at the author/publisher contract. Though this contract does not deal specifically with the concerns of illustrators, an illustrator of a picture book is generally regarded as a co-author and it is extremely useful as a detailed guide to the standard royalty contract.

10:2 WARNING. It is extremely unwise to start work on a book project before a proper contract has been negotiated and signed, and any publisher who tries to persuade you otherwise should be avoided. (This does not apply, of course, to the 2 or 3 spreads you might prepare to send round to potential publishers if you have a self-initiated project.)[2]

It is quite normal and expected for author/illustrator to negotiate a royalty contract in some detail, so don't hesitate.

How royalty contracts work

10:3 Preliminaries and Definitions

All contracts start out by defining whom the contract is between, what it is about and when it was made.

Most also include some definitions, which are indicated by initial caps, eg: 'This contract is between Jemima Jones (hereinafter called the Illustrator...)' Any subsequent mention of the Illustrator (with the initial cap) refers to Jemima Jones.

Many contracts content themselves with defining the Author, the Illustrator, the Publisher and the Work; but some start out with a whole raft of definitions, to which you will have to keep referring to make sense of the rest of the contract.

10:4 The Licence

Most publishing contracts then deal with granting the publisher a licence[3], and it is usual for the licence to be extremely wide-ranging. The publisher usually acquires an exclusive licence to publish the work, and to sub-license others to publish the work, throughout the world and for the full period of copyright. In practice this can mean that the contract may last for a hundred years or more.

This in effect means that although the illustrator retains the copyright, he/she hands over to the publisher all the powers of the copyright owner by way of a licence. The distinction is important, because handing over the copyright itself is for technical legal reasons a risky thing to do which in certain circumstances may lead to the rights becoming irretrievably lost to the author/illustrator. Copyright should hardly ever be assigned in a royalty contract.

Publishers need a very wide-ranging licence in order to sell subsidiary rights, which may form an important element in the profitability of a book, particularly a children's picture book, where co-editions are often essential to the project's viability.

10:5 However there are two situations in which the author/ illustrator may want to keep some rights:

1. If the author/illustrator is in a better position than the publisher to exploit certain rights (for instance if she/he is an animator, the author/ illustrator may want to hang on to the animation rights).

2. If the illustrations form part of a larger, pre-existing body of work. If this is the case a narrow licence allowing the publisher only the book rights (aka 'volume rights'), restricted book rights (eg the right to licence as a children's book) or even non-exclusive rights, will be appropriate.[4] Otherwise the illustrator will no longer be free to market the collection as a whole in other ways.

If the publisher subscribes to the *Minimum Terms Agreement* (see 10:68) the licence may be for a shorter period than the full term of copyright, but this is unusual, especially in the children's book field.

1. See 'Minimum Terms Agreement' (10:68).

2. See para 10:59

3. The licence is usually at the beginning of the contract, though sometimes you will find the licence for volume rights at the beginning, and the licence for non-volume rights (eg merchandising rights) further along.

4. For instance a former artist-in-residence when Shakespeare's Globe was built, licensed some of her Globe pictures to a publisher for a children's book. Unfortunately the licence was very wide, which meant that the publisher controlled all the rights for those pictures. This made it impossible for the artist to market the collection as a whole until the rights had been returned to her. In her case a licence for children's books only would have been appropriate.

Money

10:6 The Advance

The first payment an illustrator/author gets is called the *advance*. It is a sum of money paid in advance of future royalties and rights earnings, and no more will be paid until the book has earned enough to cover the money advanced.

Advances are usually paid in three stages, typically on signature of the contract, on delivery of artwork, and on publication. It is better for the illustrator to get the final slice on delivery of the artwork rather than having to wait for publication, which may be up to a year later. Consider negotiating an advance on signature, on delivery of roughs, and on delivery of artwork.

The amount of the advance is a matter for bargaining. The publisher is unlikely to give an advance of more than 60% of the book's expected first edition earnings. Some books never earn much more than the advance, and this fact should be born in mind before embarking on the project.

If the illustrator has final editorial control (see below 10:58), the advance should be payable *on delivery* and should not be returnable even if the book is never published. If the publisher has the right to reject the artwork, it should be payable *on acceptance*, but if the artwork is rejected, a proportion or the whole of the advance should be paid as a rejection fee.

10:7 Royalty payments and Rights payments

The author/illustrator gets a share of the proceeds in two forms – 'royalty' payments and 'rights' payments.

Royalty payments range from 5–15% to the author/illustrator. Rights payments, on the other hand, range from 50–90% to the author/illustrator. Why the big difference?

Royalties are a share of the profits of manufacturing an article, and are calculated either as a percentage of its retail price, or as a percentage of wholesale price (usually expressed as 'price received' or 'net receipts'). Most of the price of a book is taken up by the cost of manufacture, distribution and discounts to book-shops. Only a small part is profit to the publisher, so a royalty of 10% of the retail price may well represent 50% or more of the profit on the sale. (See cost break-down on next page).

Rights payments on the other hand are a lump sum paid for the right to use the author's/illustrator's work in some way. Thus, if a story is turned into a radio play, a lump sum will be paid for the 'dramatisation' rights. There are no manufacturing or distribution costs involved for the publisher and the proceeds are split to reflect this, the publisher taking a share varying from 10% to 50% for their expertise in organising the deal, rather like an agent.

There can be a confusion of nomenclature here because the author/illustrator may, for instance, sell the 'video rights' in a book but be paid by means of royalties on the number of videos sold, or may even get a sum of money for the sale of rights *plus* a royalty on their sales. In either case, the difference between the percentages for royalty and rights payments will apply.

Royalties and rights payments automatically take account of inflation over the years because they are based on a percentage rather than a fixed sum. Royalties expressed as 'x pence per copy' are only suitable for very short-term agreements, such as a two-year greetings card licence, where inflation can safely be ignored.

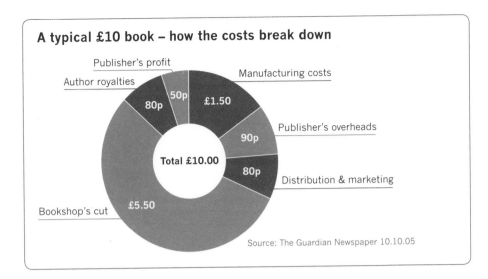

A typical £10 book – how the costs break down

- Publisher's profit — 50p
- Author royalties — 80p
- Manufacturing costs — £1.50
- Publisher's overheads — 90p
- Distribution & marketing — 80p
- Bookshop's cut — £5.50

Total £10.00

Source: The Guardian Newspaper 10.10.05

5. All the figures given here and below are for the full royalty which will be split (usually 50/50) when there is an author and co-author/illustrator.

6. Sometimes called 'net receipts', 'actual sums received' or somesuch. But beware of 'net profits' as these are too much subject to creative accounting and should never be agreed to. If the terms are defined in the contract, check that the definition is acceptable.

7. See section 10:68

Royalty Payments

10:8 Home Hardback Sales

Home sales are sales of the publisher's own edition within the UK.

Conventional publishers (as opposed to packagers) generally pay royalties based on the *retail* price for home sales. The 'normal' royalty is 10% of the retail price, though because of tight profit margins royalties for children's books can be as low as 7.5%.[5]

10:9 Export Sales of UK Hardback Edition

These are sales of the UK publisher's edition outside the UK, either in Commonwealth countries or in (English-language) bookshops abroad.

Royalties are generally calculated as a percentage of price received (i.e. the wholesale price).[6] This is because such sales are made through distributors at a large discount, and not direct to bookshops. The normal rate is 10%, which comes to about half what 10% of retail price would make.

10:10 Escalator Clauses

An escalator clause increases the royalty as the sales go up. For instance, the royalty on home sales of a children's picture book might start at 7.5% but go up to 10% after 20,000 copies, 12.5% after 30,000 copies and so on. Once the publisher is reprinting an established success, the lack of initiation costs make the whole thing more profitable, so the author should get a greater share. An escalator clause is particularly relevant if the initial royalty is low.

10:11 Small Reprints

If there is an escalator clause there may well be a small reprint clause. This reverts the royalty to its starting rate for small reprints below a certain quantity. In the case of children's picture books small reprints are not likely to be viable whatever the royalty rate. The Minimum Terms Agreement[7] says that this clause should not be invoked more than once a year without the agreement of the author.

10:12 Publisher's Own Paperback Edition

Most of the large publishers have their own paperback imprints and are likely to want to use these for a paperback edition, rather than sublicensing to a specialist paperback publisher.

The advantage of the publisher's own paperback edition is that the author/illustrator gets the full royalty, whereas if the paperback is sub-licensed the original publisher will take a cut of 25-50%. Nevertheless authors may sometimes feel that a specialist paperback publisher will sell more books. Ideally the author/illustrator should have the right to be consulted about the paperback edition.

Royalty rates on home sales are sometimes slightly lower than for the hardback edition – 5-7.5% of retail price. Export sales are usually the same as for hardbacks – 10% of net receipts. Some publishers make a distinction between 'trade' paperbacks (sold direct to bookshops) and 'mass market' paperbacks (sold via wholesalers at a discount), offering a lower royalty on mass market sales.

10:13 Royalty-Inclusive Sales

The UK publisher will sometimes manufacture an edition of the book to sell on to another publisher – for example a foreign publisher or a book club – on a 'royalty inclusive' basis. 'Royalty inclusive' means that the publisher buying the edition pays the whole royalty upfront, rather than as and when the book sells. Royalty inclusive deals are fairly common with co-editions[8], which are almost always needed to make picture books financially viable.

The usual rate for foreign edition royalty-inclusive sales is 5-6% of net receipts. For book clubs it's usually 7.5-10% of net receipts. This is less than a conventional royalty would be, though it does have the advantage that all the money comes in straight away, regardless of whether the book actually sells or not.

Nevertheless a conventional royalty is likely to be a better deal in the long run, and this is an important issue for children's book author/illustrators as the foreign co-editions will be a substantial part of the book's earnings. Good publishers will try to negotiate a conventional royalty deal and only go for a royalty-inclusive deal as second best. Because of the importance of foreign editions it's worth discussing this issue with your publisher and trying to get the rate for royalty-inclusive up to 10%.

10:14 Sheet Deals

This is really part of the 'royalty-inclusive' issue, but I've given it its own heading because of its potential importance.

Editions are sometimes sold 'royalty-inclusive' in sheet form (ie the books are not bound up).

This is very bad news for the author/illustrator, because unbound sheets will cost much less than bound books, so the royalty will be that much smaller.

In my view the author/illustrator should always be consulted about proposed sheet deals and they should not be entered into without good reason. It is sometimes possible (I have done it myself) to negotiate a veto for the author/illustrator on sheet deals.

10:15 Cheap Editions

Publishers sometimes sell cheap editions, usually of the hardback book. Royalty rates are usually the same as for the normal editions (though, of course, it's a percentage of a lower price). Cheap editions are rare where children's picture books are concerned.

8. 'Co-editions' are foreign editions printed at the same time as the UK publisher's English language edition.

10:16 Non-Booktrade Sales

These are things like Book Clubs, or books for other non-traditional outlets. 10% of net receipts is normal.

10:17 Premium Sales

You are not likely to come across this but, just in case, it means special give-away offers attached to other products. Author/illustrator should always have to give consent to this, and the royalty negotiated on a case-by-case basis. 5-10% of net receipts is usual.

10:18 Free Copies

There is usually no royalty on books given away for review or other promotional purposes.

10:19 Other Types of Payment

In a rapidly changing market you may find types of payment not mentioned here. If in doubt about what they are, ring the contracts department of your publisher and ask. If they don't know (they should, but offices all seem to have their share of imbeciles), insist that they find out and tell you.

10:20 Rights Payments

These are payments for 'subsidiary rights', and have in common that, as there is no manufacturing cost involved, the percentages paid to the author/illustrators are a lot higher. A percentage of rights payments is kept by the publisher for its services in negotiating the deal (like an agent's commission) and because their contribution in publishing and marketing the book in the first place has helped create the value of the rights.

Broadly there are two types of subsidiary rights, volume rights (ie in book form) and non-volume rights (eg merchandising).

As a general principle the rights should be controlled by whoever is in the best position to exploit them. This is usually the publisher, and it is usual for the publisher to control all the rights, but it may sometimes be the author/illustrator (for instance if the illustrator is in the animation business, she/he may wish to keep the animation/film rights, or if she/he has a lot of contacts in the giftware business, the illustrator may want to keep the merchandising rights).

Confusingly some 'rights' payments come in the form of royalties (from other publishers). But as with all rights payments, there is no manufacturing cost to the original UK publisher, who keeps a percentage on the basis described above.

10:21 Translation Rights

This means foreign language editions, published by an overseas publisher (on a 'separate royalty' rather than 'royalty-inclusive' basis). The foreign publisher will pay an advance and royalty and the author/illustrator should get 75-85%. In the children's book field some smaller publishers pay as little as 50%, which is bad news. You should try to negotiate it up. Translation rights sales form an important part of the author/illustrator's likely earnings in the picture book field, since almost all picture books are co-editions.

10:22 USA Edition

The USA edition can be so important that it is generally treated differently from other overseas editions. The USA is a very large market, and an author/illustrator may well make more from it than from the UK edition.

Publishers have a responsibility to make as good a deal as they can for the author/illustrator, and to try to avoid a royalty-inclusive deal and especially a 'sheet' deal (see 10:14). Some contracts have a 'best endeavours' undertaking by the publisher to this effect, and the author should have the right to be consulted about the USA edition.

Rates are the same as for translation rights; 75-85% to author/illustrator.

Some of the bigger UK publishers now have their own USA imprints. This does not mean that the book will automatically be published by them in America, but if it is, the royalty arrangements should be no worse than those for the UK.

10:23 Paperback Editions

If the paperback rights are sold to an outside publisher the author/illustrator should expect an advance and royalty as with the original publisher. It is sadly common for the hardback publisher to want 50% of the proceeds for their services in negotiating the deal. The Society of Authors recommend that authors should try for at least 60%, leaving the original publisher with 40%. Ideally there should be a 'de-escalator' clause reducing the amount the publisher takes when a certain sum of money has been earned, or a certain number of copies sold, though probably only well established author/illustrators will be in a position to negotiate this.

See also 'Publisher's Own Paperback Edition'.

10:24 Book Club Rights

Sometimes Book club Rights are sold on a 'separate royalty' (rather than royalty-inclusive') basis – in which case it is usual, as with paperbacks, for the author/illustrator to get 50% of the book club royalties. As with paperbacks, try for 60%.

10:25 Hardback Reprint Rights

Usually refers to library editions of books that have gone out of print, or hardback editions of books which originated as paperbacks, licensed to another publisher. 80% goes to the author/illustrator in the case of a paperback original, 50-60% if the book was originated in hardback.

10:26 Educational Reprint Rights

Seldom applicable to children's book, this means an edition, usually of a 'set text', with notes and other academic apparatus. 50% to author/illustrator.

10:27 Large Print Rights

For those with eyesight problems. Another right seldom involving children's books. Author/illustrator usually gets 50-60%.

10:28 Strip Cartoon or Picturisation Book Rights

Means what it sounds like – turning your book into a comic. 50-70% to the author/illustrator, which is rather variable. If you think it might happen, negotiate for the higher one.

9. A 'collecting society' collects and distributes money which individuals cannot easily administer for themselves. The Performing Rights Society is the best known example. It collects licence fees every time music is played in pubs, shops, on radio and TV.

10:29 Anthology Rights

An anthology is a collection of several works in one volume. Sometimes happens to children's picture books, as their short length is quite suitable for this form of publication. The usual amount to the author/illustrator is 50%. Worth trying for 60%.

10:30 Quotation and Extract Rights

A minor matter, unless you're a poet, in which case it may happen a lot. 50% to author/illustrator is usual.

10:31 Digest Rights and Book Condensation Rights

The first is a shortened version of the work in a magazine or newspaper, the second a shortened version in book form. Unlikely. 50% to author/illustrator.

10:32 Electronic Book Rights

A straight download of the book in electronic form. A potential large market in the future, but not at present. Author/illustrator usually gets 50%. In view of future potential, it might be a good move to try to negotiate it up.

10:33 Electronic Version Rights

Different from the above, it is a new version re-edited for electronic publication, potentially as different from the book form as is a film version. 50-80% to author/illustrator. If you think it a possibility, aim for the higher slice.

10:34 Reprographic Reproduction Rights

This means photocopying. Various institutions (educational, business etc) buy a 'blanket' licence to photocopy from the Copyright Licensing Agency, who in turn pass on the money to the respective collecting societies[9] for authors, publishers and visual creators. To get your share of this money as an author you should join ALCS (The Authors' Licensing and Collecting Society); as an illustrator you should apply to DACS (Design and Artists' Copyright Society) through their annual 'Payback' scheme.

10:35 Merchandising Rights

The right to turn your book (or elements of it, such as characters) into toys, cards, plates, figurines or whatever other gruesome novelty you can imagine. Author/illustrator gets 50 – 80%, and since this is a possibility, hold out for the higher figure.

If the publisher uses a merchandising agent, the agent's commission should come off the money before it is split, and the publisher's share should be at the lower end of the range.

If author and illustrator are two different people, you may need to give some thought to the split between them when it's only the illustrations (and not the words) which are 'merchandised'. It is reasonable to vary the normal 50/50 split between author and illustrator to, say, 25/75. However if the book (and spin-off merchandising) is likely to sell largely on the author's name and reputation, an equal split may be reasonable. (The same principles apply the other way round for rights which use only the words and not the pictures).

An illustrator who is already familiar with this market may wish to manage his/her own merchandising, in which case the right should be kept, or an arrangement made which varies the amount of the split according to who brokered the deal.

10:36 Dramatisation and Documentary Rights

Includes stage, screen TV. Animation is probably the most likely. For some reason the normal rate to the author/illustrator is 90%. Animator-illustrators may wish to keep these rights themselves.

10:37 Single Voice Readings

Means reading the book out on TV, radio or other public performance. Usual rate is 75% to author/illustrator.

If author and illustrator are two different people, you may need to give some thought to the split between them when it's only the words (and not the illustrations) which are used. It is reasonable to vary the normal 50/50 split between author and illustrator to, say, 75/25.

10:38 Mechanical Reproduction Rights

Usually means issuing a CD, video or tape of the work. Author/illustrator should get 50 – 75%. Can happen, so go for the higher end.

If author and illustrator are two different people, you may need to give some thought to the split between them when it's only the illustrations (and not the words) which are 'merchandised' or *vice versa*. It is reasonable to vary the normal 50/50 split to say 75/25.

10:39 Film Strip Rights

Usually happens to children's picture books. The book is photographed page by page, usually with a sound track telling the story, for use in schools. 50% to author/illustrator is normal. Why not ask for 60%?

The distinction between this and 'mechanical reproduction rights' is far from clear to me.

10:40 One Shot Periodical Rights

The right to publish the whole (unabridged) Work in a single issue of a magazine or newspaper. 50% to author/illustrator.

10:41 First Serial Rights

The right to publish extracts in issues of a magazine or newspaper *before* the book's publication date. Applies to things like memoirs of politicians, and can command juicy money if there are 'revelations'. 90% to author/illustrator, but sadly unlikely to happen.

10:42 Second and Subsequent Serial Rights

As above, but *after* publication of the book. Author/illustrator gets 50 – 75%, presumably because after publication the publisher can claim they have contributed to the value of the rights.

Essential Protection Clauses[10]

10:43 The question most illustrators and authors ask about a royalty contract is, 'are the payments fair?' But in many ways the protections that a contract should contain are more important in the long run than a few percentage points on the royalty. *All the points listed here are essential*, and authors and illustrators should insist on them, and should be wary of any publisher or packager offering a contract without these clauses.

10:44 **Undertaking to Publish**

Having acquired the right to publish the book, the publisher must guarantee to publish it, usually within 12 months of delivery of the manuscript and/or artwork. This protects against the publisher sitting on the rights and not exploiting them.

10:45 **Reversion Clauses**

Every contract should contain clauses reverting the rights back to the author/illustrator in the event of:

1. Breach of contract by the publisher not remedied within a month.

2. Bankruptcy (insolvency) of the publisher, unless for purposes of re-construction.

3. The book going out of print, and the publisher unwilling to reprint within a specified period.[11] It is very important that if your book goes out of print you should be able to get the rights back and see if you can find another publisher to re-print it.

Without these clauses the author/illustrator has no protection against a publisher who does nothing with the work or refuses to honour the contract.

10:46 **Set Times for Payment**

Royalties are usually paid twice yearly, and should be accompanied by a full statement of copies sold and other relevant details, usually in June and December. Money from rights sales should be paid within a month of receipt.

10:47 **Inspection of Accounts**

The author/illustrator (or, more usually, his/her accountant) should have the right to inspect the accounts insofar as they relate to his/her book's sales. Usually this is at the expense of the author/illustrator, unless discrepancies above a certain sum are found.

10:48 **No Assignment**

The contract should not be assignable by the publisher to anyone else without the author's consent. The illustrator/author does not want suddenly to find a new, unknown and possibly uncongenial publisher has 'bought' the right to the work. However the publisher *can* assign their business as a whole (as in a take-over, merger, or sale of the business).

10:49 **Credits and Copyright Notices**

The author/illustrator must be credited – usually on the cover and the title page. Unless the illustrator is credited on the title page, he/she may not be eligible for Public Lending Right. The author/illustrator must also be shown as the copyright holder, and her/his assertion of the moral right of paternity (the right to be identified as the author/illustrator of the work) must be asserted.

10:50 **Remainders**

Remainders are fag-ends of editions sold of cheap to the bargain book trade to clear stock. They are, alas, increasingly common. Publishers are more and more inclined these days to sell off stocks of a slow moving book. The author should get 10% of price received for remaindered books and should be notified in advance and offered the chance to buy in copies that are to be remaindered.

10. These protection clauses are important not just in publishing contracts but in any long-term contract involving payments for exploiting a copyright; for instance second right agencies.

11. What counts as 'out of print' needs to be defined. Best for the writer/illustrator is that it should mean out of print in an edition published in volume form by the UK publisher. Otherwise a few copies still hanging around in, say, the Finnish edition may prevent the author/illustrator from invoking this clause or will allow the publisher to desktop-publish a very small print-run to avoid losing the rights. In practice publisher are often happy to hand back rights if they don't have any publishing plans.

Other Important Clauses

There are a number of other clauses of importance which need to be specially watched out for.

10:51 Option Clauses

In the old days when publishers were gentlemen, they often published an author's first works reckoning to make a loss, but hoping to make a profit on later works when the author was established.

These days publishers are more likely to be accountants than gentlemen, and are generally less inclined to nurture authors and take a long term view. But they still put in option clauses, requiring first refusal of the author's next work.

The standard wording of such clauses is inappropriate for illustrators, who need to be free at the very least to take on commissioned books.

It is usually appropriate to offer an option on the next book featuring the same characters or part of the same series, but otherwise, (especially if it is offered by a small, untried publisher) it is best to delete the option clause. Illustrators who write their own books may consider a limited option clause for 'the next book written and illustrated' by themselves if it comes from a prestigious publisher in whom they have full confidence, but even this may tie them down more than they want.

At any rate the terms of any option clause should be very carefully considered beforehand. It is worth noting that the *Society of Authors* recommends the deletion of option clauses.

10:52 Competing Works

A similar issue to the option clause is the 'competing works' clause. This prevents the author/illustrator from preparing or publishing any work which 'may in the reasonable opinion of the publisher be likely to compete with' the Work. Such a clause should be struck out, or at the very least limited to a year or two, especially for specialist illustrators who need to be free to illustrate books in their specialist area to earn a living. There is an obvious danger that such books may be considered to compete by the original publisher.

10:53 Warranties And Indemnities

A warranty is a 'guarantee'. The author/illustrator is usually required to warrant that the work is libel-free and does not infringe anyone else's copyright. Libel is seldom a problem for illustrators, but copyright can be. It is very important that illustrators should take care not to copy anyone else's work, and this applies most particularly when reference photographs are used, or any reference material culled from published sources.

The author/illustrator will be expected to *indemnify* (compensate) the publisher for any breach of this warranty, which is fair enough; but many warranty clauses go on to say that the author/illustrator indemnifies the publisher against any *alleged* breach of the warranty. This part of the clause should be deleted.[12] It means that if someone claims (alleges) that the work is an infringement of, for instance, their copyright, the publisher may choose to pay them off and then look to the author/illustrator for the money – even if the alleged infringement was not in fact a infringement at all.

12. Wording for such clauses vary. Typical would be 'or arising out of any *claim alleging* that the Work constitutes in any way a breach of this warranty' (my italics). The words to look out for are 'claim' or 'allege'.

13. Provided the book is not time-sensitive, publishers will generally choose to re-schedule the publication date. But they don't have to.

10 | Royalty Agreements | page 95

Publishers point out that such claims are nearly always settled out of court so that the breach cannot be proved, and fighting each case in court would be ruinous. It's a fair point, but putting the whole burden on the author/illustrator is not the answer.

This is a hard conundrum to resolve. Some publishers have provisions by which the publisher and author/illustrator jointly appoint a lawyer to advise them, which is an improvement. But in my opinion the best option is for the author/illustrator to strike out the 'alleged breach' phrase. Then if the publisher decides to settle, and feels that the author/illustrator is to blame, they can seek their indemnity on the grounds that the author/illustrator *was* in breach. This gives the author/illustrator a chance to defend her/himself if appropriate.

10:54 Delivery

There will be a provision for a delivery date. The illustrator should make sure that this is realistic and allows enough contingency time, especially if the delivery clause says that 'time is of the essence' (meaning that the author/illustrator will be in breach if the deadline is missed even slightly.)

In the case of books originated by the author/illustrator, if the delivery date is not met, the publisher generally has the option of not publishing the book, and paying no more of the advance.[13] The author/illustrator should be able to keep the money advanced so far, usually with the proviso that when the book is finished the publisher shall have first opportunity to renew its offer to publish.

If the book has been commissioned, or if 'time is of the essence', it is quite likely that the publisher will expect return of the advance if the delivery date is not met and it decides not to publish.

If you suspect you may have difficulty with a deadline, the best thing to do is to notify the publisher straight away.

Other Clauses

The following clauses are generally not contentious, and are included for the sake of completeness.

10:55 Actions For Infringement

There is usually a clause empowering the publisher to take legal action at its own expense to protect the copyright and allowing them to join the author/illustrator's name to the action (though at the publisher's sole cost).

10:56 Free Copies

Most contracts allow the author/illustrator 6 free copies and the right to buy further copies at trade price (though not for resale). If you would like more free copies, ask.

10:57 Production and Promotion

The publisher usually expects to have control over the design, production and promotion of the book. You may wish to be consulted over some of these matters. If so, ask for a clause to that effect. The publisher will want the last word, however.

Since the late 19th century books have been printed on acidic paper which gradually deteriorates and will, if left untreated, eventually self-destruct. There is no reason why picture books should not be printed on acid-free paper, and a clause to this effect, though unusual, seems to me a good idea.

Miscellaneous Issues

10:58 Commissioned or uncommissioned? Who has the last say?

There are usually slightly different expectations about editorial control and other matters depending on whether the book is commissioned or not.

If the author/illustrator, either as a team or as a single person, originates the book and presents it to a publisher for consideration, then the publisher will be more inclined to let the author/illustrator have the last say about how the book should be written and illustrated. The publisher may offer suggestions, and may offer to publish the book only on condition that certain changes are made; but in essence the book is the author's, not the publisher's. In this situation you would not expect to find a requirement for approval of the illustrations or text, nor a rejection fee proviso. If the publisher eventually decides not to publish, the advance paid up to that stage is kept by the author/illustrator, who is then free to offer the book elsewhere.

If the publisher has *commissioned* the book it may well want to approve the illustrations (or text) and have the right to ask for changes. In this case you might find there is a set rejection fee, or an arrangement that in the event of rejection the final part of the advance is not paid. The illustrator needs to be satisfied that the rejection fee is high enough. Getting a 50% rejection fee for a single magazine illustration is not too serious. A 50% rejection fee for something that has taken 3 months to complete is a different matter.

10:59 Choosing a publisher

If you have originated a book you will want to find a publisher. Potential publishers generally expect to see about 3 finished double page spreads, roughs for most of the remaining pictures and a complete text – no more. Remember, the publisher may want to change the format, so don't invest a lot of time in finished artwork at this stage.

Generally speaking the large, well-known publishers offer better terms than smaller ones. The relationship with your publisher is long-lasting, so you want to be sure the publisher is reputable and likely to treat you fairly. If in doubt, look at their back-list and if necessary contact other authors or illustrators it publishes. (You can write to them c/o the publisher if you can't track them down any other way).

10:60 Development agreements

Publishers sometimes commission an illustrator to do two or three double-page spreads and perhaps some roughs for a text, from which they hope to sell enough foreign editions to make a viable project. In this case they will typically offer to pay a flat fee for the 'development' work. If they get enough co-editions and the project goes ahead, they will then sign a full contract.

In this situation it is essential that there should be an indication of what sort of royalty agreement the illustrator can eventually expect. Otherwise the illustrator may do the development work, only to be presented later on with an unacceptable contract for the whole job, which creates a difficult situation for both sides.

A formal contract for development work is not necessary. A letter from the publisher setting out the outlines of the proposed royalty agreement is enough.

This precaution is particularly important when dealing with small publishers or book packagers (see below).

10:61 Book Packagers

Book *packagers* are a phenomenon that arose in the 1970s. A book packager does everything that a publisher does except store, distribute and publish the book under its own imprint.

Typically book packagers initiate projects, hire a writer and illustrator, get the book printed and then sell the whole edition on to a conventional publisher or to a retail or other outlet. The attraction of this arrangement for the packager is that it requires less capital. The packager gets paid for the edition at about the time it has to pay it's printer and creative suppliers, and does not have to wait for the book to sell in the shops before it get its money back and makes its profit.

When book packaging first started, a lot of people with entrepreneurial flair but little knowledge of publishing went in for it. Some of the worst publishing contracts I have ever seen date from this period. Since then the *Book Packagers Association* has improved matters and packager contracts are nowhere near as bad as they used to be. Nevertheless there are some issues to look out for when dealing with a book packager.

1. Book packagers are not suitable if you are looking for a publisher for your own self-initiated project. You will be better off with a conventional publisher.

2. Book packagers often offer royalties for Home Sales based on the wholesale, not the retail price. This is substantially less (see para 10:9). Try to bargain up.

3. Percentages offered for rights (see para 10:20) are low, usually no higher than 50% for any right. Try to bargain up.

4. Some of the protection clauses may be missing in a packager contract, especially the Inspection of Accounts clause (see 10:47). The Book Packager's Association's model contract omits this clause (or did when I last saw it) but it is worth knowing that the clause is included as an optional extra in the *appendix* to their model contract. There is nothing optional about an Inspection of Accounts clause. Always insist on all the protection clauses.

5. Book packagers are the worst offenders when it comes to not agreeing the contract before you start work. I have known illustrators find themselves half way through a job before the contract is sent, let alone agreed. Do not allow this to happen.

6. If offered development work, make sure you have an outline of the eventual full contract and are happy with it before you start.

7. Book packagers are particularly prone to ask for unrealistic deadlines. Make clear at the start how much time you need and leave plenty of contingency time. Rushed work is often bad work, which benefits nobody.

10:62 Small Publishers

Many of the issues I mention in connection with book packagers also apply to some small publishers.

10:63 Who gets Royalties

Some publishers offer a flat fee for picture book illustrations. This is likely to be in the case with compilations (eg children's reference books with several illustrators involved), educational books, puzzle books and the like, and other titles at the cheaper end of the market initiated by the publisher. Flat fees are also more common with book packagers. Flat fees are normal for children's novels (as opposed to picture books).

The licensing of flat fee commissions for book illustration is discussed in section 4.

Books initiated by the illustrator or by an author/illustrator team should always be on a royalty basis. In general the illustrator will earn more in the long run from royalties than from a flat fee.

10:64 Public Lending Right

Public Lending Right is a payment made to the author and illustrator of a book every time it is loaned in a public library. Because books linger on in libraries long after they are out of print, you may still be making a modest sum from PLR for some years after a book has stopped earning royalties.

To be eligible you must be a resident of the EU, Iceland, Norway or Liechtenstein. Your name must be on the title page of the book, or you must be entitled to a royalty. If you are the illustrator, but not the author of the book, you must agree with your author how the PLR should be split between you (or between all the contributors if there are more than two) and then both must submit an application. The usual shares for a children's picture book is 50/50; for a children's novel (with approx one picture per chapter) 80/20 in favour of the author seems to be generally acceptable. If your author is dead or untraceable, you can still register for your share.

More details from PLR, Richard House, Sorbonne Close, Stockton-on-Tees , TS17 6DA, or on-line from www.plr.uk.com.

10:65 Literary Agents

If children's books form a substantial part of your practice, consider getting a literary agent to handle your book work. More information about literary agents can be found in section 'Agents'

10:66 Advice

Unless you are very confident, it is wise to get advice about royalty agreements. *The Association of Illustrators* gives free advice to members as does *The Society of Authors* (see below).

10:67 Short-Period Royalty Contracts

The same principles apply to short royalty contracts which last for say 5 years (eg merchandising contracts) as to conventional publishing contracts. However the protection clauses, whilst desirable, are not all as vital as they are with long contracts, and royalties can be based on a fixed price of x pence per sale, as inflation is not much of a problem.

10:68 Minimum Terms Agreement

This is an agreement drawn up by the Society of Authors and Writer's Guild, setting standards for royalty contracts. Its most significant provision is to limit the publisher's licence to 20-30 years (or some other period by negotiation), with the right to a review in good faith of the terms of the contract every 10 years at either party's request. A few publishers subscribe to it, though I have never seen it mentioned in the context of children's picture books. It's a good idea, though it has rather fizzled out in the last few years.

Useful Books And Organisations

10:69 The Writer's and Artist's Yearbook

Published annually by A and C Black, this long standing reference book is essential. Amongst other things it lists literary agents who handle illustrators.

10:70 The Writer's Handbook

A recent rival to the *Writer's and Artist's Yearbook*, aimed exclusively at authors and contains an 'authors' rating' review of many publishers. Less all inclusive than the Writer's and Artist's Yearbook, but rather livelier and perhaps more informative if you are looking for a publisher.

10:71 Publishing Agreements (Ed: Charles Clark)

An excellent and detailed guide to publishing agreements, aimed mainly at writers and publishers, though there is a (rather unsatisfactory) flat fee illustration agreement. The model author/publisher royalty agreement though is excellent and the notes very informative. This is essential reading for any illustrators who write their own books and intend to negotiate their own contracts. Published by Unwin Hyman.

10:72 Character Merchandising by John Adams

This book costs an eye-watering £148 last time we looked, and is very technical. However, for illustrators heavily into character merchandising and wishing to understand how to look after their own interests, it's probably a good investment. Also available *Character Merchandising in Europe* by Heijo Ruijsenaars. Still expensive at £90. You could try ordering these from your local public library.

10:73 The Association of Illustrators

Offers free advice to members on royalty contracts, pricing and other legal conundrums, and publishes this handbook.

10:74 The Society of Authors

An authors' organisation, open to illustrators, which offers advice on publishing contracts – though it's aimed at writers, not illustrators. Children's book illustrators wishing to make contact with authors might consider joining and attending the children's book group. Annual subscription similar to the AOI.

10:75 The Authors Licensing and Copyright Society (ALCS)
Distributes money to authors (not illustrators) if their book is photocopied. This is most likely to happen after the book has gone out of print, especially to books which are used in schools. Registering with ALCS costs nothing and is worth doing.

10:76 The Design and Artists' Copyright Society (DACS)
Distributes photocopying money (and other funds) to visual creators through its 'Payback' campaign every year. You can ask to be put on their list for a claim form, or download one from the web.

10:77 Royalty contract checklist for books
Use this checklist to make sure you have considered all the important points in a royalty contract.

Licence
• What rights does the publisher control?

• Any rights you want to keep?

Advance
• How much? What proportion of UK first printing earnings? Will it be a disaster if there's no more money?

• To be paid when? (Avoid 'on publication' if possible)

• Non-returnable in case of rejection/non-publication?

Royalties
• Calculated on retail price for Home Sales?

• Escalator clause?

• Special arrangements for USA edition?

• Does publisher have own paperback imprint? If so what arrangements for paperback publication?

• Distinction between 'trade' and 'mass' paperback?

• Bound book, sheet or film sale payments reasonable?

Rights
• Amounts for rights sales reasonable?

Design and production?
• Special conditions you want to impose? (Acid free paper? / Design?)

Author warranties and undertakings
• Delivery date realistic, plus contingency time?

• Warranty exemption for reference material supplied by publisher?

• 'Breach' only or 'alleged breach'?

• 'Similar or competing works' restrictions?

• Option clause?

Protections (publisher undertakings)
- Undertaking to publish?
- Reversion for breach, out-of-print, bankruptcy?
- Set times for payments?
- Inspection of accounts?
- No assignment?
- Credits (right of paternity) including title page and cover?
- Period before remaindering permitted?

10:78 Royalty payments checklist

Royalties
- **Home hardback**   7.5 – 10% of retail price
  (plus ecalator to 15%).

- **Export hardback**   7.5 – 10% of price received
  (plus escalator) or 50% of home hardback royalty.

- **Small reprint** – Generally used to bring escalated royalties back to base rate.
  Rates below base rate should be resisted.

- **Hardback cheap editions** – Same as home and export hardback.

- **Publisher's own paperback** – Usually slightly less than hardback edition.

  - *Home sales*   6 – 8% of retail price

  - *Export sales*   6 – 8% of price received
    Escalator desirable.

  - Some publishers distinguish between trade and mass market paperbacks.
    Few publishers these days license to specialist paperback publishers
    (eg Penguin).

- **Non-booktrade sales**   7.5 – 10%
  (Special editions not through normal book trade – eg supermarkets).

- **Premium sales**   c. 5 – 10%
  (eg copies given away with other goods and services). A royalty to be agreed.
  Author's consent should be obtained depending on circumstances.

- **Royalty inclusive book club**   10% of price received.
  Applicable where book club is buying edition from publisher, not
  manufacturing themselves (in which case see below).

- **Royalty inclusive overseas sales**
  Where foreign publisher is buying manufactured copies or sheets from
  UK publisher.

  - **Hardback**   7.5 – 10% of price received.

  - **Paperback and other cheap editions**   5 – 6% of price received.

  - If possible, get veto on sheet deals, or promise of consultation, or higher
    payments – (though this is not common).

Rights percentages

All percentages are the author/illustrator's share. The publisher's cut is for their services in negotiating the deal · i.e. they are acting as agents. Beware · some publishers try to cut down on these percentages.

- **Publication in USA** – Author should have right to consult on this.
  Publisher should undertake to try to get US royalty on US published price,
  the best deal.   75 – 85%

Minority interest books may have to make do with 'royalty inclusive overseas sale' (see above).

- **Translation rights** (This means foreign editions).   75 – 85%
  More likely to be dealt with on a royalty inclusive basis
  these days, except in countries with a big market.

- **Sub-licenced paperback**   50 – 75%
  (eg to Penguin, rather than publisher's own paperback).

- **Hardcover reprint** (eg library edition).   50 – 60%
  unless from paperback original, in which case 80%

- **Electronic book**   50%
  (ie a straightforward version of the book in electronic form).

- **Electronic version** (ie an interactive version).   50 – 80%
  The distinction is important. (See Clark p 23*).

- **First serial rights**   90%
  (ie newspaper serialization before publication in book form).

- **Second/subsequent serial rights**   50 – 75%
  As above, but *after* publication in book form.

- **Dramatisation and documentary** (On stage, TV, film etc.) 90%

- **Quotation and extract**   50%

- **Anthology**   50%

- **Digest rights** (eg Readers Digest)   50%

- **Digest book** (eg condensed book)   50%

- **One shot periodical**   50%
  (Complete book in one issue of periodical).

- **Educational reprint**   Conventionally 50%
  but worth asking for more, especially if likely to happen.

- **Large print version**   50 – 60%

- **Book club on royalty basis**   50 – 60%
  (eg where Book Club manufactures).

- **Single voice readings**   75%

- **Merchandising rights**   50 – 80%
  This is potentially important with children's books, and should be negotiated
  on the high side, especially if the publisher is using a merchandising agent
  (see Clark p 20*).

- **Mechanical reproduction**   50 – 75%
  (eg CD cassette etc; anything that's not electronic.

- **Film strip rights**   50% is normal,
  (Applicable to childrens' picture books) but try for   75%

- **Reprographic rights** (This means photocopying).   50%
  by collective agreement. Not negotiable.

- **Print handicapped/braille**   Gratis.

* Publishing Agreements, ed Charles Clark, 5th edition (Butterworths).

Illustration by Adam Graff

11 Going to law

When all else fails, the last resort in resolving a dispute is to go to law. This should be avoided if possible, because even the cheap and informal Small Claims procedure described here consumes a great deal of time and emotional energy. But if you have to go down the legal route, here's how to do it.

11:1 Small Claims

At the time of writing, the Small Claims procedure at the County Court is available as of right when the sum involved is £5,000.00 or less[1]. However, the County Court has discretion to use the small claims procedure for larger sums if both parties agree. It also prefers 'debt' claims – that is claims involving payment of money owed. Most claims can be cast in this way, since even if you are asking for return of a/w or taking a copyright infringement case, you will be asking for financial compensation either as the penalty or as an alternative. The small claims procedure is cheap because lawyers do not need to get involved (in fact small claims courts prefer the parties to represent themselves, and some forbid the use of solicitors). This means that the cost of any legal expertise used by the other side will not be awarded against you if you lose the case. The only costs that are permitted (and can be awarded against the losing party) are the court fee (starting at 10% of the amount claimed up to a maximum of £120)[2], witnesses' expenses if they are needed, plus the cost of using an expert witness (see below), and out-of-pocket expenses.

11:2 A warning letter

The first step in the small claims procedure is to write a 'letter of claim'. This is simply a short letter telling the person you are in dispute with that you intend to take them to court unless they are prepared to settle the matter within a set time. You should also set out fully (but without irrelevant detail) the basis of your case.

Let us suppose that you have been commissioned to produce a magazine illustration without a formal agreement about the licence the client is buying. You reasonably assume they will want 'one use' in their magazine. (If you were sensible you would have issued a 'one use' licence as soon as you got the commission, but in this case you didn't). You send in your invoice, the client sends a cheque, but you find you cannot pay in the cheque without first signing a statement on the back which gives the client the copyright. Your letter of claim might read:

Re your payment ref 1234567 my invoice no 123
'I cannot accept the condition you have set for payment. Our agreement as I understood it was that I was to illustrate the article 'How to Be a Millionaire' for one use in your magazine, and this was the basis on which I undertook the commission. There was no demand at that stage that I should assign copyright, and if there had been I would not have agreed to the assignment.

'I must therefore ask you to issue a new cheque without this pre-condition within one week, failing which I shall start proceedings in the county court for recovery of the sum due.'

Your letter should be short, to the point and business-like. It should *not* be emotional, rambling or in any way a rant. Bear in mind this letter will form part of the documentation seen by the court, and a reasonable and businesslike attitude on your part will help your case.

11:3 Drafting your claim

It is important to think about the way you will state your case in the 'statement of claim' (see below). This is the first thing the District Judge will see, and it helps if it contains the legal essence of your case without a lot of padding and unnecessary detail. An example might be:

1. On Sept 8th 2006 I was commissioned by Grabbit Magazine Group Ltd (The Defendant) to produce a half-page colour illustration for an article entitled 'How to Be a Millionaire' in the October issue of their magazine 'Money News' for a fee of £250.00.

2. There was no specific agreement as to the licence to be transferred. However the commission was for one use to illustrate their article, and this is the basis on which I agreed the fee. *(Your legal argument here is that there was an 'implied'[3] licence).*

3. The illustration was completed and accepted, but the defendants now require that I assign copyright in the illustration to them as a condition of payment.

4. I ask the court to order that the defendants pay the agreed fee without this precondition. (In more legal terms you might say 'I ask the court to order specific performance of the original implied contract').

If you are a member of the AOI, you may be able to get help drafting your claim. Otherwise, if you feel you are having difficulty with it, consider consulting a solicitor to help you with this task, but bear in mind that you will not be able to reclaim this cost if you win. Whilst a well-drafted claim is helpful, it is certainly not necessary to use legal language in your statement of claim.

11:4 Starting the case

Assuming the other side do not respond to your 'letter of claim' the next stage is to start court proceedings. Go to your local County Court (County Courts are listed under 'Courts' in your business phone book and are usually open from 10am – 4pm during the week), and fill in a claim form stating the nature of your claim as you have drafted it. You will need to know the name and registered address of the company you are acting against (or name and address of the person, if it's not a company).

Alternatively you can start a claim online at www.moneyclaim.gov.uk, if the only remedy you are seeking is payment of money due.

You are entitled to claim interest on money owed to you. If you want to do this write in the 'particulars of claim' section of the claim form *'The claimant claims interest under section 69 of the County Courts Act 1984 at the rate of 8% a year from (date when the money became owed) to (date of claim form) of (total amount) and also interest at the same rate up to the date of judgment or earlier payment at a daily rate of (0.00022 x the amount of your claim)'.* Phew!

1. In rare cases the court may decide that the issues are of such legal complexity that a small claims procedure is not suitable. However this is unlikely to apply to most cases (I have never known it happen).

2. At the time of writing. Check with your local County Court or visit www.hmcourts-service.gov.uk for up-to-date fees.

3. See 8:8

11:5 When the defendant receives your claim

The court will send your claim to the other side, who must then admit the claim or enter a defence (and/or they may enter a 'counterclaim' of their own).

If they admit the claim, the court will order what you have asked. They may well admit the claim simply because they feel it's less trouble than defending the case.

If they enter a defence and/or a counterclaim, you may be asked to complete an 'allocation questionnaire' which helps the court decide how to deal with the case (how to 'allocate' it). You will have to pay an allocation fee of £100 (at the time of writing). You can claim this from the defendant if you win.

11:6 What it's like at court

The case will be heard at the nearest court to the defendant if the defendant is an individual, not a company. This can be a nuisance, but cannot be avoided without an application to court to request a change of venue (with good reasons).

When you get to court you will be put in a waiting room with others who have cases at the court. There will be an 'usher' present (sometimes gowned, but wigs are not worn), who is in charge of the arrangements, and checks everyone in. The defendants will also be there, if they turn up. If you find this intimidating, bring someone along with you for moral support. They can also come with you into the actual hearing. If you wish, you can be represented by a friend or colleague, but there is seldom much point in this as you will end up having to do most of the talking yourself anyway, when the district judge asks you what happened.

You will probably have to wait a while before your case is called. It's a bit like a hospital appointment. The fact that your case is 'listed' for 10am just means that it is on a list that starts at 10am, and if it's a long way down the list you may have a considerable wait. The list of cases will be posted up somewhere, or you can ask the usher how far up on the list it is.

11:7 The hearing

The District Judge will set the date for the hearing or may even decide to determine the case without a hearing. In exceptional cases the Judge may order a preliminary hearing before the full hearing.

When your case is called you will be directed to the court room. You will usually find some rows of benches (often with desk slopes in front of them to write on) facing the Judge's (usually raised) desk. It is the convention, but not essential, that the plaintiff (or claimant) sits on the left, the defendants on the right.

The Judge may ask you about the nature of the dispute and ask the defendants about their defence (or counterclaim), and how many witnesses (including expert witnesses) each side expects to call; this is to give him an idea how long the case will take.

When telling the Judge about your case, start at the beginning, keep calm, try not to be emotional and keep to the point. The Judge will be making notes, so give him/her time to make them by leaving appropriate pauses and not speaking too quickly. If you feel so nervous that you dry up, just explain that you are nervous. The Judge will usually try to help you.

If for any reason you feel you need to alter the details of your claim, you can ask leave to do so. This will usually be granted at the preliminary hearing but not at the full hearing.

4. Known as 'contemporaneous notes', these are considered good evidence.

5. For how to value artwork, see 3:22

The Judge will then urge the parties to settle out of court, and order 'disclosure' of documents (which means each side must let the other see any documents they intend to use in evidence).

It is acceptable to address the District Judge as 'Sir' or 'Madam', though you don't have to use any title. If at any point you absolutely need to interrupt, your best tactic is to get to your feet and wait for the Judge to ask you what you wish to say. Do not do this without a *very* good reason though. You will usually get a chance to make your point if you wait.

A date will sometimes be set for the full hearing (if this is a preliminary hearing), or may be notified by the court later.

11:8 Settling out of court

If there has been a preliminary hearing there may be an opportunity immediately afterwards, if you are feeling up to it, to see if the other side is interested in settling. However, don't allow yourself to be intimidated. If necessary say you will consider their proposals and communicate with them later.

11:9 Preparing for a full hearing

If you have not managed to reach a settlement after a preliminary hearing (if there is one), the case will go to a full hearing. In the meanwhile you need to gather your evidence. Or you need to do this earlier if there is no preliminary hearing.

You need to have copies (one for you, one for the defendant, one for the district judge) of any relevant documents you intend to use in evidence. These may include the original brief (any emails, faxes etc), any notes made by you *at the relevant time*[4] – even scribbled notes; and possibly your roughs, artwork etc if appropriate. Copies should be sent to the defendants at this stage.

You may need to arrange for witnesses to come to the court to support your case, or an expert witness to give evidence about, for instance, trade practice, or about the value of artwork.[5] If an important witness cannot come on the day set for the hearing, you can ask the court to alter the date. Your witnesses should also bring any documentary evidence they may have for what they say (for instance if they are giving a valuation of artwork, any documentary evidence to support their opinion, such as records of similar sales, or invoices for sale of artwork) and these should also be sent to the defendants.

You may wish to call a witness who is unwilling to attend because he/she is employed by the defendant, or is a friend or fellow illustrator who does not want to fall out with the defendant. In this case you *can* ask the court to issue a witness summons. This means the witness *must* come to court. Having no choice in the matter may be less embarrassing for him/her if they have some relationship with the defendant. On the other hand, a hostile witness may not help your case.

11:10 Expert witnesses

An expert witness is a person with particular expertise who can give evidence if appropriate. A plumber may be called as an expert witness, for instance, in a case involving a faulty plumbing job. In illustration, the most likely type of expert witness might be an agent, experienced fellow illustrator or gallery owner.

The usual procedure if you need an expert witness is to commission a written expert report. If this supports your case and you intend to use it in evidence,

you must send it to the other side. Ask if they are prepared to agree it, to save the expense of the expert witness appearing in court.

An expert witness is entitled to charge for the report and for appearing in court. The courts have set fee limits which you can claim for this against the other side if you win your case, currently set at £200. You will need to find out what these are. The Judge may allow larger sums to be awarded if he/she feels it is justified. However you will have to pay this money up front initially, and will only get it back if you win.

Expert witnesses should be prepared to back up their opinion with evidence if they can. This is particularly important in cases involving trade practice, pricing of artwork or pricing of original illustration. Judges sometimes take a layman's attitude to pricing and are inclined to be reluctant to accept the idea of different fees for different uses without good evidence. This evidence also must be disclosed to the other side.

11:11 The full hearing

This is similar to the preliminary hearing (if there was one), but likely to be longer, since the Judge will ask each side questions to sort out the facts, and will examine the evidence.

Remember to speak slowly and calmly, and keep an eye on the progress of the Judge's note-taking, to give him/her time to get it all down.

The District Judge will also take evidence from any witnesses. You will be given the chance to question the defendant and their witnesses yourself. Don't do this unless there's some point you want to bring out. Don't be tempted to go in for TV style cross-examination for its own sake – it's very unlikely to be successful.

You will get a judgment (or 'award' as it is called in a small claims case) at the end of the case, and the Judge will explain his/her reasons for it. Very occasionally you may get a written award at a later date, but this is rare and only happens if the Judge needs time to think over what he/she has heard. If you are awarded money by the Judge, this will be paid into the court, and forwarded to you.

11:12 If in doubt

If at any time you have questions you want to ask, approach one of the ushers. They are generally helpful.

11:13 If the defendant has not turned up...

... the court will automatically give an award in your favour. Though this sounds like good news, it usually is not, since the defendant can ask for the judgment to be set aside and a new hearing held. This is usually granted, especially if the defendant can give some half-way decent reason why he/she failed to appear.

11:14 When not to go to court

Although the small claims court is inexpensive and relatively informal, you should always ask yourself if it is worth going to court.

Does the defendant have any money? If not, the case is probably not worth pursuing.

A case will probably take about six months from beginning to end, and a lot of your time and emotional energy, so if the sum involved is modest you may be better off writing it off to experience. The stress of going through a court case can be considerable. In addition, if the defendant is really unreasonable, they may try not to pay. If that happens you will have to go through a whole extra process to extract the award from them, taking yet more time and energy (see below).

On the other hand sometimes a mere threat of court action will produce results, and you have the option of starting a court case with a view to pulling out if it looks like getting more protracted than it's worth. In fact only a very small percentage of legal disputes actually go to court. Most are settled in correspondence between solicitors.

Only you can decide this. Weigh up the pros and cons, and try to make your decision on dispassionate business principles – don't let your heart rule your head.

11:15 Enforcing payment

If you win your case but the defendant doesn't pay up, what next? There are various steps you can take.

- Start by writing and pointing out that a judgment against them for failing to pay will affect their credit rating. If this fails you can...

- Get an order from the court that they (if an individual) or their company attend court for questioning as to their means (*'Application for order that debtor – or officer of debtor company – attend court for questioning'*).

Having found out what they're worth you can use various devices to get your hands on it...

- Get an order from the court for a bailiff to seize their goods (*'Request for warrant of execution'*).

- Get an order from the court to force their bank (or anyone else who holds money for them) to pay (*'Application for a third party debt order'*).

  or, if they are an individual, not a company, you can...

- Ask the court for an attachment of earnings (*'Request for attachment of earnings order'*).

You can even – though hopefully you won't need to go this far – ask the court for a *'charging order on land or property'* or for a *'charging order on securities'* (stocks and shares etc).

Forms for all these applications can be got from your local County Court or on-line from www.hmcourts-service.gov.uk.

11:16 Formal court cases

A full-blown court case with lawyers is so expensive (five figures at least, perhaps six) that it is out of the question for most illustrators. Even if you win, you will not get all your costs back |(typically only 70%) and if you lose you will have to pay the other side's costs as well as your own. Even with a strong case, it's possible to lose, especially if you get the wrong judge.

If you have a dispute worth a lot of money, a possible solution is to see if a solicitor will pursue it on a 'no win, no fee' basis. Even if this is possible, be aware that you will have to pay an insurance premium to cover the possibility of losing.

It can sometimes be worth threatening a court case through a solicitor in hope of getting a settlement. The danger is that you can get sucked in, feeling at each stage that if you spend just a little more money you may get a result. In the end you have spent so much that you feel you've got to go ahead in hope of recouping it. It's very easy to get sucked into this sort of situation, though your solicitor has a duty to tell you if the costs are going to be disproportionate to the value of the case. If you do go down this route be clear in advance at what point you will call it a day and *stick to that decision*.

11:17 Alternative dispute resolution

There are a number of mediation and arbitration[6] procedures you can consider. Though cheaper than a full-blown court case, these are not all *that* cheap. A typical case with CEDR[7], one of the longest established commercial *mediation* organisations, is likely to cost £4,000 at the time of writing, though there are cheaper alternatives. Note, however, that both parties have to agree to mediation and, unlike a binding arbitration, it may not produce a result. At the time of writing the government is trialing various 'proportionate' dispute resolution schemes, but the scene is changing so fast it is pointless to give specific details here. If you are interesting in following up this possibility, use a web search in UK pages for 'alternative dispute resolution', 'arbitration' and 'mediation' and see what's on offer.

6. An arbitrator will act in the same way as a judge, though more informally. A mediator, on the other hand, merely facilitates an agreement between the parties without judging between them or, usually, even suggesting solutions. Mediation is a skilled process, and requires training.

7. www.cedr.co.uk

Appendix Further Reading & Index

Appendix A

Rights Grabs

A:1 When the Association of Illustrators first came into existence, one of the principal aims of its founders was to change the law (as they assumed it existed) which said that commissioners of illustration automatically owned the artwork; a practice that was then widespread, indeed taken for granted.

In the event, the AOI discovered that whilst this was true under the Copyright Act of 1956 for photography, it was not true, and never had been, for illustration. Armed with this nugget of legal knowledge, the AOI set about changing the practice and by 1980 had largely succeeded. Nowadays no one seeks to challenge the principle that illustrators, not commissioners, own the artwork, unless otherwise agreed.

Illustrators now face a different challenge, *'Rights Grabs'*; that is to say, attempts by commissioners to use their superior industrial strength to force creators to assign their copyright, waive their moral rights and, in some cases, hand over the ownership of the artwork as well. This is not a wholly new phenomenon. Half-hearted attempts to get copyrights have existed for a number of years (notably from IPC and a few educational publishers) but in recent years the problem has become considerably worse, and is now a major threat to the livelihood of illustrators (and many other creators).

A:2 Why it's important to resist rights grabs
Money
The whole economy of illustration works on the basis that clients buy different types of licence, and pay according to the extent of the use they want. This breaks down if it becomes normal for clients to acquire copyright, since as the copyright owner the client can use the image for whatever it wants, and even sell it on to third parties.

Loss of control
It's bad enough to have your image used without restriction by the original client, but once copyright is transferred there is nothing to stop it being sold on to, say, an image bank. In that case the original illustrator will find himself potentially competing with (and being undercut by) his own work, or may find his image being used in a context which he objects to. The illustrator himself will have no right to reproduce his own image once copyright has been assigned.

Loss of future earnings
If the illustrator retains the copyright, he can on retirement exploit his past work in image banks if he wishes. He is also entitled to payment for secondary uses, such as photocopying.[1]

Distortions
Rights Grabs inevitably include a waiver of moral rights, including the right of integrity. So the illustrator may have his work changed, distorted or used out of context, and will have no redress.

Ownership of Artwork
Many rights grabs also include ownership of the artwork by the client. This makes little sense at a time when so much artwork is digitally created, but is a major consideration for many illustrators.

When the illustrator objects to a rights grab, the publisher will say that they need it for administrative convenience, and that no one has objected before. None of this is true

Illustration by Lasse Skarbövik

1. Payed through DACS' 'Payback' system. I myself got £700 last year from this source, £1500 the year before.

A:3 Why do commissioners want to grab rights?

Fear and loathing of new technology.

Prof Hugenholz in a paper presented at a conference at NYU in 2000 said:

> "We see the total transfer of rights becoming standard business practice, not out of necessity, not to facilitate enforcement, not for logistic purposes, not for reasons of efficiency or legal security, but as a symptom of existential insecurity, because the publishers have no idea what the future has in store for them, and for the works created by 'their' authors."

Big conglomerates

There are few independent publishers left these days. Most belong to some larger corporation, who, unlike independent publishers, employ their own in-house lawyers. The lawyer's job is to protect the interests of his employer, regardless of the cost to others. Drafting a 'fair' contract is a difficult thing to do. By far the easier and safer option as far as the legal department is concerned is a thoroughly one-sided contract, provided it can be enforced. According to Lionel Bentley, Reader in Law Kings College London, the routine legal advice given to publishers is: 'You have the power. Take as many rights as you can. Hoard them. Then if something happens you will get the windfall.'

The shock of the new

The first shock was the then 'new' Copyright Act of 1989. It changed the position of commissioned photographers and made them, for the first time, owners of their copyrights unless otherwise agreed. Some commissioners have been trying to claw this back ever since, and illustrators, though their position has not changed, have got caught up in the process.

The second shock was much more serious; the digital revolution. CDRoms and the internet presented new forms of publication and new means of transmission, and publishers found that, not only did they have no idea how these would work out, but they had none of the rights necessary to exploit the new markets. Furthermore they could not be sure the rug would not be pulled out from under their business models, putting them all out of a job. The fate of the music industry after the growth of file-sharing was a dire warning as far as paper-based publishers were concerned. This perhaps comes under the heading of 'Fear and loathing of new technology'.

The legal background

A:4 Contract law

In the UK and most of Europe it is a principle of contract law that *'Contracts that are entered into freely and voluntarily shall be held sacred.'*

Courts will not reopen contracts because they are 'unfair'. There is no doctrine of equality of bargaining power in UK law.

As Dr Fred Breinersdorfer, Chair of the Writers Union, Germany, says of this principle, 'In practice freedom to negotiate requires equal strength. Without that, what we have is a free fox loose in a free chicken run.'

A:5 Copyright law

Globally, there are two competing cultures of copyright. The Anglo-American *copyright* model, and the much more creator-friendly European *Creator's Right* model. In the Anglo-American model (found in the UK, USA, Ireland and most commonwealth countries) copyright is essentially a utilitarian property law, invented as an unfortunate, pragmatic necessity to give publishers an incentive to publish and creators to create. Macauly (1800-1859) called it 'The evil of copyright' because he regarded it as a monopoly 'a tax on readers for the purpose of giving a bounty to writers'. Furthermore, so far as Anglo/America is concerned, copyright is a mere commodity, which can be bought and sold like any other.

A:6 *Creator's Right*

The ethical underpinning of Creator's Right ('Droit D'Auteur', 'Urheberrecht', 'Diritto D'Autore' all mean the same thing) is different. It is an '*a priori*' innate *natural* right belonging to flesh and blood authors, like the right to life, liberty, free speech. As it says in the *Universal Declaration of Human Rights:*

> 'Everyone has the right to the protection of the moral and material interests resulting from any scientific, literary or artistic production of which he is the author.'

In some jurisdictions, therefore, author's right cannot be sold (Germany) or cannot belong to a corporate entity but only to a flesh and blood human (France).

It is thus no co-incidence that all the recent improvements in law for creators – the extension of copyright to 70 years, the introduction of Moral Rights, the 'not for profit' limits on 'permitted acts' and, most recently, the introduction of Resale Right for fine artists – have come from the European Union, often after opposition from the UK government.

A:7 Reasons to be cheerful

The rights grab situation is pretty grim as I write, but there are some signs that give creators reason for optimism.

First of all it should be remembered that many attempted rights grabs are 'try-ons'. That is to say, the commissioner routinely issues a rights grab contract initially, on the basis that some creators will be too naive or too nervous to oppose it. This is tedious, but easily overcome by requesting their 'non-standard' licensed contract. This situation applies to most magazines and many educational publishers.

The first determined attempt at mass rights grabs came in the advertising industry, immediately after the introduction of the 1989 Copyright, Design and Patents Act. In an attempt to claw back the rights which the new act had given to photographers, and because of an exaggerated fear of the consequences of moral rights, as large number of advertising agencies wrote to their creative suppliers, some enclosing a pound coin[2], demanding that the creative suppliers agree to assign all their future and past copyrights in work commissioned by the agency, and waive moral rights. If they did not, they would not be employed by the agency.

Dire though this threat seemed, nearly all advertising illustrators are represented by agents; and the agents, a determined bunch, simply refused to go along with this demand. Faced with determined and widespread opposition the agencies had no choice but to retreat. Now they present no problem, and are, indeed, one of the easiest categories of client to deal with.

2. For the reason for the pound coin, look up 'consideration' in the index.

3. For a suggested way of dealing with this see section 4.

Something similar happened recently with BBC worldwide. For some time they had succeeded in enforcing rights grabs with their photographers for many of their magazines. These magazines dealt with subjects such a cookery, where there was a ready choice of creative suppliers who were more or less interchangeable. But when they decided to launch a fashion magazine they found that no such thing would be possible, for the simple reason that the fashion photographers, many celebrities in their own right, would not put up with it; so they had to back off.

It is clear that faced with determined opposition, commissioners *will* back off. Even if the opposition comes from a minority of suppliers, it can still be enough to force the commissioner to draw up a second, more creator-friendly contract, for such contingencies. Once such a contract exists, the door is half open to persuading them to adopt this as their 'standard' contract.

A:8 German law

Of all the national versions of Droit D'Auteur, this is the most creator friendly, thanks mostly to recent Creators' Law of January 25 2002, which I really think creators should mark and celebrate in some way every year like May Day.

Urheberecht – 'creator's right' – the German version of copyright starts from a strong position from the creators point of view. Rights Grabs as we know them are impossible. This is because not only are Moral Rights inalienable, but Economic Rights as well. In Germany a creator cannot assign copyright. Deals can *only* be made by licence. 'Creator's Right' is seen as an innate right of the creator, no more able to be sold than, say, the right to life.

Anyone who's had any dealings with, say, OUP will know that this is not the whole solution. Their first line of defence against a refusal to assign copyright is to ask for a licence which turns out to give them just about all the benefits of copyright (except the right to get all the photocopying money)[3].

Like most European copyright laws, certain protections apply to interpretation of contracts eg:

> Work cannot be licensed for means of transmission as yet unknown (it can in the UK) and: any licence which does not specifically enumerate uses is interpreted narrowly.

> On January 25 2002, in face of vociferous and well-funded objections from industry, Germany passed a Creator's Law which set out to deal with the fundamental contract law problem facing any freelance creator – inequality of bargaining power.

In effect this law modifies the 'freedom of contract' doctrine.

1. Every Creator has the right to appropriate payment and the legal right to have payment adjusted if not appropriate.

2. The courts can establish what payment is 'appropriate'.

3. All sides have the *right* to negotiate fixed minimum rates, which must be followed by the courts as a basis for awards. (Not just non-existent in the UK, but actually illegal under 'Fair Trading' legislation).

4. If the associations representing each side cannot agree, either side can call for arbitration.

5. *Bestseller clause:* Where made to forfeit rights for a lump sum payment, if the work makes a big success, creator can apply for a top-up.

6. Right of revocation after 2 years – if licences are not adequately exploited.

7. Right of revocation for 'change of conviction' though as this requires indemnity, it is not often relevant.

In other words what we have in Germany is a tamed fox in the chicken run.

Some similar, though less radical, changes have also been proposed in Dutch law. In the long run, a strategic aim of UK creators should be to have a similar 'creators' law' introduced in the UK.

Appendix B

Rejection, cancellation and change of brief

B:1 Rejection fees

A rejection fee is paid when the client considers the illustration to be unsatisfactory and does not intend to use it.

The customary rate for rejection fees is:
At rough stage	25%
At artwork stage	50%

The client retains no rights in rejected artwork, except a general right to restrain further exploitation if the artwork is based on the client's rough.

In law if a person orders, say, a table to be made in a specified style and to specified measurements, then if the table has been made as instructed the commissioner is bound to pay for it, whether he/she likes the result or not. If the instructions have not been carried out correctly, he/she may have to pay nothing, or may have to pay some lesser sum, depending on the degree to which the work has not been properly performed.

But when artwork is rejected it is often difficult to assign the blame wholly to one side or the other; either because the rejection is caused by subjective opinions about quality, or because details of the brief are recollected differently by each party.

This is the reason for the 50% rejection fee system. It saves time in long drawn-out disputes about intangible or unprovable matters.

The 50% rejection fee apportions the financial penalty equally between client and illustrator, and operates on a swings and roundabouts principle. In some cases the client may feel that he/she has had the worse of the bargain because the work was sub-standard; in others the illustrator may feel that the real reason for the rejection was that the client had had second thoughts about the type of illustration wanted.

Before artwork is rejected, the illustrator should, as a matter of good practice, be given an opportunity to rectify the fault and should be notified within a reasonable time of the rejection and the reason for it. This, however, is not a specific term of the AOI Model Terms and Conditions, since there are cases in which the standard of the work is so poor that the client may have no confidence in the illustrator's ability to fulfill the brief.

1. It can be some other percentage. Some illustrators charge more for new clients than for the client who commissioned the image in the first place.

B:2 Cancellation fees

Cancellation fees are payable when the commission is cancelled through no fault of the illustrator. The customary rates are:

Before rough stage	25%
On delivery of roughs	33%
On delivery of artwork	100%
At intermediate stages	pro rata for work completed.

The client retains the rights in the cancelled work that he/she would have acquired if the project had gone ahead.

The reason for the 25% cancellation fee before work has begun is that in setting aside time to do an agreed commission, illustrators have to turn down other work, so that cancellation even before work has begun can cause financial loss.

B:3 Change of brief

Any alterations or extra work caused by a change of brief should be subject to extra payment to be agreed. However, no extra payment is due for changes caused by the fault of the illustrator.

Appendix C

Re-use fees

C:1 There is no absolute necessity for a method of calculating re-use fees. They can be bargained, like any other fee, on a 'what the market will bear' basis. However, some clients suspect that they are being held up to ransom when asked to pay a re-use fee (taking the view that they are being asked to shell out again for something they have already paid for), so a logical method of calculation can help overcome this.

Nor is there any generally agreed method for calculating re-use fees, though the two I suggest here are widely (but by no means universally) used. The first is the '50%' rule, which sounds simpler than it is; the second is the method agreed by the AOI, the AOP (Photographers) and the two organisations representing the advertising agencies and their clients, thanks to the efforts of the Advertising Art Buyers' Committee, which negotiated and championed this agreement.

If you find it hard to understand these two methods, you are not alone. Many people do. Persistence and re-reading will be rewarded, however. They are not as incomprehensible as they may at first seem.

C:2 The 50% rule

The basic idea is simple enough. The illustrator charges 50%[1] of the usual fee for a re-use of existing artwork. Some only apply this when the re-use is wanted by the original commissioner, charging a higher percentage, or whatever the market will bear, for a new client.

For example, suppose a client commissions an advertising illustration for £2,000, then decides it wants to use the same image for brochure covers.

In that case the illustrator would ask for 50% of the normal brochure cover price of £1000, thus –

Original advertising use	£2,000.00
50% for brochure cover re-use	£500.00 (first use price £1,000.00)
Total	**£2,500.00**

That all seems straightforward enough until you come to apply it the other way around. Suppose the brochure cover is the original use, and the advertising is a re-use.
Then you get –

Original brochure use (full price)	£1,000.00
Advertising re-use (@ 50%)	£1,000.00
Total	**£2,000.00** – which is £500.00 less.

The solution is to charge full price for the-higher paid, most expensive, use, 50% for the other uses, then deduct the price of whichever use the client first bought (this is where many readers will part company with me). E.g. –

Suppose the client commissions the brochure first (and pays £1,000.00 for it) then wants to re-use the image for advertising. The calculation then goes:

Advertising use (the most expensive) at full price	£2,000.00
Brochure use at 50% of full price	£500.00
Total	**£2,500.00**

From this you then deduct whatever sum the client has already paid – in this case £1,000.00, the fee for the initial brochure use.

Whichever way this calculation is done, the illustrator gets paid the same amount. The only difference is the sum the commissioner has already paid for the first use.

C:3 Advertising art buyers' committee re-use guidelines

If you thought that was complicated, this is even more so. It was agreed between the Advertising Art Buyers' Committee and the Society of Artists' Agents, and a similar method is used for photography. It is recommended by the AOI and the Society of Artists' Agents, and widely used as a starting point for negotiations in advertising. Because it is based on charging a full fee for the re-use, plus multipliers for extra territories and extra time, it can result in very high fees. For this reason it is not strictly adhered to if the client's budget simply will not stretch and the illustrator is content to settle for less.

The 'CUR'

The method is based on a constant called the 'Commissioned Use Rate' (CUR). All other uses are shown as a percentage of the CUR.

The CUR, on which all other usage percentages are based, is the price for a 48 sheet poster for 1-2 years in the UK. This is 100% CUR. When re-using the illustration the new fee should be calculated by establishing the CUR and taking the relevant percentage. The table below shows the relevant percentages. You will see that they are not precisely fixed and in themselves leave room for negotiation.

Media (in all cases for 1-2 yrs, uk only)	**CUR**
Consumer magazines	50-100%
National Press	50-100%
Regional Press	25-50%
Trade Press	25-50%
National 48 sheet poster	100%
Regional 48 sheet poster	40-75%
Other posters	30-65%
Point of Sale	25-50%
Direct Mail	35-75%
Internet/World Wide Web	TBN
CD Rom	TBN
All Use Licence (UK only)	300-500%

Extra territories

If the client wants additional territories, they are calculated as a percentage of the UK fee, as follows:

Territory	**% of UK fee**
Single country	20-50%
Europe	200%
Europe inc Eastern Europe	300%
North America	200%
USA only	150%
Canada only	50%
Africa	100%
Asia (excluding Japan)	75%
Asia (including Japan)	175%
Japan	100%
Oceana/Australia	100%
Worldwide	500%

Longer period

All these prices are based on 1-2 years. If the client wants longer, the first extra year is 50%, subsequent years 25%.

Example

It might help to show how this works out in practice. Suppose you do a brochure cover illustration, for which you charge £1,000, which the client then wants to use for regional press advertising. Brochures come under the general heading of 'Direct Mail', so let's assume that from the range given you think 50% CUR is about right. That tells us that the CUR is £2,000, and the regional press rate, at 25-50% of that is between £500 and £1,000, depending on the region.

C:4 Two-stage pricing

Some illustrators get round all this by quoting in two stages: one a price for doing the work, then secondly, on top of that, a price for the usage licence. In the case of a re-use, they just charge the price for the licence, not the price for doing the work. This doesn't solve much, because you still need some way of working out the prices for different licences. It also has the disadvantage that it doesn't work for a lot of editorial work, which is so poorly paid these days that once the client has paid a fair price for doing the work, there's nothing left over in the budget for the licence. However that's the fault of the appalling prices being paid for editorial work these days, not the fault of the method. It works well enough in advertising, and makes a good bargaining point for those jobs where the work involved in actually creating the image is greater than usual.

Appendix D

The Doc Martens case

R. Griggs Ltd v Ross Evans (2003) EWHC 2914 (Original case)
R. Griggs Group Ltd v Ross Evans and others (2005) EWCA (Civ) 11 (Appeal)

D:1 Why this case is important

The case concerns a designer who created a logo for (as he thought) point-of-sale use only. The client claimed that no such restriction existed, and that although there had been no specific agreement, the copyright should be assigned to it. The case went against the designer.

In the words of Robert Lands (of Finers Stephens Innocent) reporting the case in the AOI Journal '...the AOI have already encountered clients of AOI members pointing to this case in arguments over copyright' and he adds 'Illustrators should no longer rely on silence as being to their advantage, *especially when creating anything which could conceivably be adopted as a corporate logo or trading identity*' (my italics).

The original judgment was appealed and was upheld (that is to say the appeal was dismissed), which means that the judgment is now binding on the lower courts. That being so, it is important to understand what exactly the judgment said and what it did not say.

It is also an interesting case study in its own right, giving an insight into how courts think, especially when dealing with evidence and with 'implied' or 'equitable' transfers of rights.[1]

D:2 The facts of the case

A good many years ago a company called R Griggs and Co, who made industrial footwear, got a licence from a Dr Maertens to manufacture his boots, originally designed for elderly German ladies with foot problems. They marketed these as industrial footwear. In the course of time, with a slightly anglicised spelling, Dr Martens boots became an unexpected fashion success.

The boots carried two logos; the original *Dr Martens* logo (which was licensed to R. Griggs) and R. Griggs own *AirWair* logo. In 1988 R. Griggs, worried by the

1. See 8:8.

2. 'Equity' is a legal term meaning, more or less, 'fairness in the circumstances'.

Appendix C | Appendix D | page 125

possibility of one day losing the licence from Dr Maertens, decided to combine the two logos, hoping in that way to make it more difficult to split the brands. They commissioned a small advertising agency Irwin Jordan Ltd to design the combined logo, and the agency in turn commissioned freelance designer Ross Evans to do the work.

It would seem that the logo work was commissioned in with a lot of point-of-sale work, and the designer did the work on the assumption (not discussed) that the logo was intended for point-of-sale use in the UK. When he discovered that it was being used as a logo throughout the world, he took the matter up with R. Griggs, presumably with a view to extra payment, claiming that had he known it was to be used as a world-wide logo, he would have charged more.

However, negotiations with R. Griggs broke down, and some time later he assigned the copyright in the logo to an Australian company, Raben Footwear. Quite why Raben Footwear wanted the logo is unclear. The original judge suggested that they 'appeared to have no desire to own the logo other than to spite R. Griggs'.

At this point R. Griggs went to court claiming that the copyright in the logo should have been assigned to them in the first place by implication – a so-called 'equitable assignment'[2] – and could not therefore have been assigned to Raben Footwear. R. Griggs won their case, Ross Evans and Raben Footwear appealed, and the original judgment in favour of R. Griggs was upheld.

D:3 The evidence

The court had to decide, first of all, on Ross Evans' assertion that the work was commissioned for point-of-sale use in the UK, that if he had known the logo was wanted for more than UK point-of-sale he would have charged a lot more, and that consequently it was an implied term of the contract that the only licence granted to R. Griggs was for point-of-sale use in the UK.

Evidence was presented in:

• A letter from the agency to Ross Evans,

• The agency's order for the job and

• Ross Evans' own invoice to the agency.

The letter from the agency to Ross Evans in 1987 runs as follows: *'In response to our recent discussions, I am pleased to confirm that we would be happy to commission creative work from you. As agreed, this would be paid for at a standard rate of £15 per hour. I am sure we both realize that some work may need to be charged at less than this rate, whilst other operations can equally be charged at somewhat more'.*

Whilst this backs up Ross Evans' general point that some work is charged more or charged less according to use, the phrase *'somewhat more'* (my italics) does not indicate a vastly greater payment.

The agency's order for the job was headed *'Visuals for Griggs UK point-of-sale material.'* As well as the logo, it included several other images for point-of-sale material such as swing tickets. This tends to support Ross Evans claim that he regarded the work as point-of-sale. It seems to me, though, that 'point-of-sale' and 'logo' are mutually exclusive. An alert illustrator given a job under this heading would certainly query it, since a logo confined only to point-of-sale use in the UK seems an unlikely proposition.

Ross Evans' own invoice for the job referred to *'Griggs Updated UK point of sale material designs including: client briefing, headline writing, logo "combination" designs, highly finished visuals for client presentation'*. This certainly shows that Ross Evans at the time considered the use to be UK point-of-sale, though it has no contractual force as a licence since the invoice was sent after the contract has been made. Its value is evidential only.

To me and to many illustrators, the implication from all this is that Ross Evans assumed the work he was doing was point-of-sale, and most illustrators would expect a substantially higher fee for a logo to be used in the usual way than for one for point-of-sale use only.

The judge, however, found that on the balance of probabilities[3] Ross Evans had *not* been underpaid. He said that the evidence was that at Irwin Jordan, a small advertising agency, 'some margin (was) allowed for the exigencies of a particular case, but not much'. He also found on the evidence presented that Ross Evans did not usually bargain for remuneration based on the value of a campaign to the client. I have not been able to see the full judgment in the lower court, so do not know all the evidence that was presented, but it seems possible that in fact Ross Evans had in the past seldom, if ever, negotiated a substantially higher fee than his standard £15 per hour[4].

On the 'point-of-sale' issue he said that, whilst Ross Evans' work was for point-of-sale, he did not think that Ross Evans had given much thought to exactly what rights the client was acquiring. He also found that the amount of 'skill and labour' involved in creating the new logo was not great – essentially combining two pre-existing logos, a concept proposed by the client – and argued that therefore the commercial value of the logo was not the result of Ross Evans' work, but of its use by R. Griggs on their very successful boots.

Having decided, in effect, that the amount of the payment to Ross Evans, and other evidence, did not of itself imply a restricted licence under contract law principles, the court turned to what it believed would be an appropriate implied licence.

D:4 Legal issues

When a contract does not specify the rights transferred, the general rule a court applies when deciding what transfer of rights might be *implied* is summed up by Paul Harris of Hammonds in his commentary on this case;

> 'A court will not imply a grant of some right in a contract, particularly an assignment of copyright, lightly.'

But in this particular case Deputy Judge Peter Prescott commented:

> 'It seems to me that when a freelance designer is commissioned to create a logo for the client, the designer will have an uphill task *if he wishes to contend that he is free to assign the copyright to a competitor.'* (My italics). 'This is because, in order to give business efficacy to the contract, it will rarely be enough to imply a term that the client shall enjoy a mere licence to use the logo, and nothing more. In most cases it will be obvious, it will 'go without saying', that the client will need further rights. He will surely need some further right to prevent others from reproducing the logo.'

He quoted the principles for considering implied transfers of rights set out at length in a previous case *Robin Ray v Classic FM plc (1998)*. Among these were:

> Circumstances may exist when the necessity for an assignment of copyright may be established. [...] These circumstances are, however, only likely to arise if the Client needs, in addition to the right to use the copyright works,

the right to exclude the Contractor[5] from using the work and the ability to enforce the copyright against third parties. Examples of when this situation may arise include:

a. where the purpose in commissioning the work is for the Client to multiply and sell copies on the market *for which the work was created* (my italics) free from the sale of copies in competition with the Client by the Contractor or third parties;

b. where the Contractor creates a work which is derivative from a pre-existing work of the Client, e.g. when a draughtsman is engaged to turn designs of an article in sketch form by the Client into formal manufacturing drawings, and the draughtsman could not use the drawings himself without infringing the underlying rights of the client.

The list of principles ends with the following:

The licence accordingly, is to be limited to what is in the joint contemplation of the parties at the date of the contract, and does not extend to enable the Client to take advantage of a new, unexpected profitable opportunity.

Example a) is, on the face of it, extremely problematic for creators, implying that a client who needs to protect himself against competitors needs to have the entire copyright assigned to him. It seems to me to be not only self-contradictory, but also to contradict the last principle. It is self contradictory because it protects the Client against the possibility of competing works in the market for which the image was created by giving the Client the whole copyright – that is, the right to exploit the image in all sorts of other markets – a right which was not contemplated at the time of the commission, thus contradicting the principle that the licence '...is to be limited to what is in the joint contemplation of the parties at the date of the contract'. By this doctrine, a person who buys an exclusive licence to sell t-shirts bearing a certain image, would then be able to claim the copyright (and thus acquire all sorts of other rights) on the ground that he needed to protect himself against rival t-shirt manufacturers. This is clearly a nonsense, and cannot have been the intended meaning of the judgment.

Furthermore, example a) makes more sense in the context of the 1956 Copyright Act, under which an exclusive licensee could not sue in their own name only, but had to join the name of the copyright owner to the action. It makes less sense after 1989 when the new Copyright Act came into force, and for the first time exclusive licensees were able to sue under their own name without reference to the copyright owner.

But the judgment does make sense in the context of the facts of this particular case, even if one feels (as I do) that Ross Evans was entitled to more money than he got. In this case:

• The contract was created before the new Copyright Act 1988 (so with a mere licence R. Griggs would have had to join Ross Evans as copyright owner to any action they took to protect their logo).

• A logo was concerned. Even if the court had taken a minimalist approach, they would have had to give R. Griggs a licence for the whole period of copyright for all uses throughout the world, since it is the nature of a logo that these are rights required to give 'business efficacy' to the contract. Such a licence virtually amounts to the same thing as copyright and in this case does not confer any extra rights other than the right to sue under their sole name.

---

3. The standard of proof required in a civil action. 'Beyond a reasonable doubt' is only required in criminal cases.

4. It seems to be very hard to persuade judges of the legitimacy of greatly different 'use' fees. A very similar case arose in 1987, the so-called 'Black Cat' case (Peter Warner v Gestetner and others) in which I was called as an expert witness. Peter Warner charged £225 each for designing 4 motifs showing cats in silhouette. He claimed that the verbal agreement was that they would be used by clients Gestetner in a trade show, and that there was a possibility that one would be turned into a logo, in which case a further fee would be negotiated. In the event one was turned into a logo, but no further fee was negotiated, and the design group concerned denied that any such agreement had been made. I gave evidence that £225 was a reasonable fee for below-the-line use, but much too little for a logo. There was also a contemporaneous note made by Peter Warner, and his licence terms (given at invoice stage and so too late to make a contract) all of which tended to support his claim. However the judge found, rather against the evidence I thought, that no such agreement had been made. His view was that the £225 was an adequate fee for the logo. In retrospect I think Peter Warner's side should have presented more hard evidence of different use fees (in the form of previous examples, which certainly would have been available). Such evidence would have made it harder for the judge to rely on his own 'common sense' view about what was an appropriate fee.

5. By which is meant the freelance contractor ie Ross Evans.

- Ross Evans had not simply asked for more money, he had purported to assign the logo to a 'rival' company.

- The 'new' logo consisted of two pre-existing logos combined (example b).

D:5 Conclusion

Whilst this case *may* apply to create an equitable assignment of copyright in other cases involving a logo[6] even after 1989, I do not think it can be extended to create an assignment of copyright in a wider context, and any attempt by clients to claim that it does should be resisted.

However, the principles set out in the case may create a wider licence than the creator would like in other instances, where the use that the client is commissioning is left in doubt. In such cases it is especially important to make sure that a licence exists in writing, agreed at the time of the commission.

The judgment also highlights a weakness in the existing copyright law. As things stand, an exclusive licensee has his exclusivity in respect only of the use he has commissioned. An exclusive licence to use an image for a brochure cover, for instance, only protects the licensee against the image being used by someone else as a brochure cover. There is no protection against it being re-licensed as, say, a book jacket. The convention (set out explicitly in the AOI's standard terms of trade) is that the creator undertakes not to re-licence the image for any use that would be detrimental to the original client's business; but this undertaking is only as good as the probity of the illustrator, since if a third party gets a licence from the illustrator in good faith and without knowing about the undertaking, they may be entitled, in equity, to hang on to it. The original commissioner could get damages from the illustrator, but this would not stop the second use.

A final lesson from the judgment is the importance of supplying good supporting evidence for different use fees in this sort of case. As in the 'Black Cat' case (see footnote 4 to D3), it seems that judges find this hard to accept.

Appendix E

Association of Illustrators Members' Code of Conduct

1. **Members shall conduct their business competently and act at all times with integrity and honesty.**

2. **When accepting a commission, members should ensure that clients are aware of the extent of the rights they are purchasing. If no contract has been supplied by the client, members should provide written confirmation of engagement, which includes this information.**

   Licensing illustration and sending terms of trade are normally thought of as a protection for the illustrator; but it is in the interest of both sides that terms are clear. The client is entitled to know what rights they have bought, and to have the information in writing for future reference. The illustrator has at least as much responsibility as the client to ensure that this happens.

3. **Members shall treat all information relating to their client's business as confidential.**

Advertising jobs, both below and above-the-line, can be a particularly sensitive area in this respect, especially at the presentation stage when the agency/design group may well be pitching against others.

4. **Members who intend to be away from their normal place of work for more than a full working day should inform any client for whom they are currently working.**
This is a good rule to adhere to, even if the illustrator is working on a long job and not expecting the client to be in touch. It can be very unnerving for a client to find they cannot contact an illustrator and cannot find out when he/she will be back at work.

5. **Members shall not subcontract work without the agreement of the client except in areas of illustration where this is customary (eg storyboards).**
This has sometimes been a problem in the area of realistic illustration, where styles are less distinguishable, Clients, quite rightly, object.

6. **Once the client has approved a rough, members should not make significant changes at artwork stage without prior approval.**
The artist may feel that there is an obvious improvement that can be made, but from the client's point of view, commissioning illustration is already an unpredictable process, and sudden changes at artwork stage will only add to the client's nervousness about the outcome, and may affect their willingness to use illustration in the future.

7. **In accepting an open brief, members must be prepared to make radical changes at rough stage if the client so requires.**

8. **Artwork should be of similar style and standard to that already approved in the artist's portfolio, unless otherwise agreed with the client.**

9. **Members may not charge extra fees for alterations which are the fault of the artist, nor for trivial alterations; however members may charge a reasonable fee for significant alterations which were not in the original brief.**

10. **Members must use their best endeavours to deliver work on time and if they anticipate any delay, must inform the client at the first opportunity.**
By the nature of things illustrators cannot subcontract work, and a great deal of money may hang on delivery of a piece of work, particularly in advertising. In principle, once an artist has agreed to do a job, he/she can be sued for failing to deliver on time if this has damaged the client, unless the artist is actually incapacitated by illness or some other unavoidable cause.

11. **Members must not licence artwork to a third party during the currency of an existing licence unless agreed with the client. In addition, advertising illustration should not be re-licensed to a third party after the expiry of the licence, if such action is likely to be detrimental to the client's business.**
The chief purpose of the licence is to prevent the client from using the work for uses it has not paid for. An image should only be re-licensed to third parties once the original client has finished with it, and in the case of advertising special care is needed. This does not apply to areas such as card design, where simultaneous licensing for different products is customary.

6. One might argue that it only creates an assignment of copyright if the commission was before 1989 because that was when the 1988 Copyright Act became active and changed the position of exclusive licensees, but from the creator's point of view this is a fairly academic point, since the licence implied would anyway be so all-inclusive as to amount virtually to the same thing.

12. Members working on advertising or promotional illustration should not knowingly work simultaneously for clients who are in direct competition with one another without the agreement of both. In the case of conflict, members should accept the commission of the first comer.

13. Members must not act recklessly to endanger the relationship between an intermediary (e.g. design group or advertising agency) and its client. In particular, members should inform the intermediary before taking any legal action against its client and give it a reasonable opportunity to settle the matter itself.

Conduct to other artists and to agents

14. Members shall not set out to copy the work, or imitate the style of another illustrator, and may not accept commissions to do so. However, emulation of, and influence by another artist is permissible.

15. Members must at all times bear in mind the reputation of their agency and the other artists represented by it and act accordingly.

16. Members must honour agreements with their agents and in particular any agreement about exclusivity of representation. If a potential client refuses to deal through an agent, members should accept the commission only after obtaining the agreement of their agent.

17. Members should not discuss money or deadlines with a client if represented by an agent unless otherwise agreed.

18. Members must inform their agent if they intend to be away from their normal place of work for a full working day or more.

19. Members must inform their agent immediately of any anticipated delay in delivery.

Speculative work

20. Members should not undertake speculative work without a fee, except in the case of self-generated work.

This code is issued by the Association of Illustrators as an advisory standard of ethics and professional conduct for its members.

Appendix F

The Society of Artists' Agents Code of Ethics

The SAA together with the Association of Illustrators abide by the following Terms and Conditions for the commissioning of artwork:

Society of Artists Agents Code of Ethics

1. **Agents** are reimbursed by a commission charged on the work handled by them and agreed with the individual artists. As Agents they do not act as commissioners (principals), and copyright remains with the Artist unless it has been specifically assigned to a Client with that Artist's consent.

2. **Agents** shall negotiate the terms of any assignment, with the Artist having the right, before commencement, to reject any assignment where the terms are found unacceptable, or which they consider unsuitable. The Society is opposed to any client requesting work on a speculative basis because of the inherent risks of exploitation in such circumstances, and no member Agent shall accept work on that basis. It is realised that there are times e.g. when clients are pitching for new accounts, when limited budgets make the fixing of a realistic fee impossible, but in those instances, at the least an honorarium and/or expenses should be paid.

3. **Artists** will provide agents with samples of artwork, which from time to time are necessary for the purpose of securing assignments. All such artwork samples remain the property of the Artist and shall be returned promptly, subject to availability, after the termination of any agreement concerning representation. The Agent, while using their best endeavours to have work returned by clients, is however not responsible for work not returned by such clients.

4. **On assignments** secured by the Agent, the Agent shall be entitled to a commission based on an agreed percentage. The Artist shall be informed of the fee paid by the client and the percentage commission on every assignment. On house accounts there may be a reduced or nil percentage. House accounts are defined as those accounts that have been obtained by the artist prior to the date of their representation and listed in a schedule drawn up at the commencement of such representation.

5. **Before commencement** of the work there shall be a written instruction, order or job acceptance form provided by the Agent, detailing proposed fee, delivery dates and all other relevant details.

6. **The agent** shall make prompt payment of any and all fees collected on behalf of the Artist at mutually agreed intervals. Statements showing all assignments, client's names, fees paid, expenses incurred, the dates of payment and the amount of the Agent's commission, will be supplied upon request. All of these form part of the initial agreement between the Artist and Agent.

7. **The agent** is aware that the Artist, together with his/her financial adviser, has the right in the event of a dispute, to inspect the accounts in respect of work done by that Artist at the place of business, during normal business hours, after giving reasonable notice. Such inspection to be at the Artist's own expense, except if an error exceeding £100 in their favour is found.

8. **No agent** may knowingly directly approach an Artist already represented by another Agent with the view to representing them. If a member Agent is approached by an Artist represented by another Member Agent they may provide details of the services that they offer, but they may not offer any inducement. If an Artist does decide to join a new Agent it is imperative that the original agent is informed by the Artist promptly, and it is considered both a courtesy and advisable that they discuss the new arrangements.

9. **Representation** may be terminated by either party by giving thirty (30) days written notice. If the Artist receives any assignments after that termination date, originally instigated by the original Agent, commission shall be payable on that work for a period not exceeding one year after the date of termination. Irrespective of termination date, any second rights/extensions of licenses relating to assignments dealt with by the original Agent would be negotiated and dealt with by the original Agent. It would be expected that

any other form of enquiry for the Artist would be referred on. Any and all Agent to Illustrator representation agreements/contracts to be subject to approval by the SAA membership (if requested) and to comply with the SAA approved recommended agent-illustrator contract guidelines/parameters.

10. **Should any member** who resigns, or who has their membership terminated, wish to re-apply for membership, they may do so after six months and only after satisfying the criteria for membership and agreeing to abide by the Constitution and Code of Practice. Such an application will be treated in all respects like a new application and the decision of the SAA Main Committee, in consultation with the membership, will be binding.

11. **All discussion** and business of the Society, whether in closed or in open committee, is to be treated by members as confidential and not for general release unless specifically agreed. Casual discussion of the affairs of the Society can prove damaging to the Society and all members will be expected to behave with discretion in this respect. Any member found to be in breach of confidence may be asked to explain their conduct to the SAA Main Committee.

12. **Any agent** not conforming to the Society's Code of Practice will be required to appear before the SAA Main Committee to explain their conduct, and if such conduct is proven, may form the basis for that agent's membership of the Society to be terminated. Refusal to provide a satisfactory explanation will also be grounds for termination.

13. **The Society,** in common with many other professional bodies, recognises particular potential threats to artists deriving from the use of royalty-free images, and whilst the Society does not bar or prohibit entirely responsible and reputable member agents from some engagement with the sector, the Society shall require all member agents to exercise a particularly high level of caution and moderation with regards to any dealings that it (and the artists it markets) may have in the sector. Member agents shall be required by the SAA Main Committee (upon request) to account to the Society at any time, in written and/or oral form, detailing any and all interests that they may have in the sector, within 7 days.

    The Society shall also have the right to seek statements from artists marketed by the said agency, detailing the artists commercial view regarding all aspects of their dealings in the royalty-free sector. If the Society is satisfied with the schedule of interests in the sector presented by any existing or prospective member agent (and the artists marketed by the agency in question), then the Society shall conduct a full membership vote regarding admission or retention of the particular agency, and a majority of 60% of the membership shall be required in order to admit or retain the said agency.

14. **The Society** is committed to working for the advancement of illustration and illustrators as an art and commercial form in conjunction with The Association of Illustrators and other related trade organisations and societies in the United Kingdom and worldwide.

1. This general rule does not apply to the work of illustrators in employment.

2. This has been the case since about 1977, largely as a result of the advice given to the AOI by the Whitford Committee. For instance, a draft document put out by the Business Design Group of the Chartered Society of Designers says, under the heading *Intellectual Property*, "Original illustrations normally remain the property of the illustrator unless specifically purchased."

Appendix G

Ownership of artwork

G.1 What is the law?

Clients who are not used to commissioning illustration sometimes suppose that they automatically become the owners of any artwork they commission. However, this is not the case.

In law, copyright and the ownership of the physical artwork are two separate properties, and the sale of one does not imply that the other has been sold with it.[1]

For instance, if you buy a Picasso painting to hang on your wall, you do not own the copyright in it just because you have bought the physical artwork. The copyright remains with Picasso · or his heirs in this case. Conversely, a commissioner of illustration, who is buying the right to reproduce the work (that is to say, a usage right stemming from the copyright), does not become the owner of the physical object.

The point was put succinctly by Mr Justice Whitford when evidence was being given at the Whitford Committee on Copyright and Designs Law: "Unless the illustrator agrees to give the original to the commissioner or client it remains his property. The fact that someone has bought the copyright does not entitle him to own the original artwork."

G.2 Customary practice

It is now widely accepted throughout the industry that illustrators own their artwork and most clients return it on demand or as a matter of course.[2]

It is, of course, open to clients to seek to acquire ownership of the artwork by special agreements, and the illustrator may be willing to sell for an agreed price.

G.3 Why do illustrators need their artwork?

Firstly, illustrations have value for sale as works of art, and some illustrators make a significant part of their living by this means.

Secondly, illustrators need good examples of their work for their portfolios, for submission to competitions, exhibitions and annuals and for self-promotion generally. Printed versions are inadequate for most of these purposes, and the ability to promote his or her work is essential to an illustrator's career.

Thirdly, illustrators are reluctant to see their cherished works disappear into a client's storage, often in the end to be thrown away. In the past, many illustrations which would now be very valuable have been destroyed in this way.

G.4 What rights does the Client have?

The client is entitled to have access to the artwork in order to reproduce the work.

Obviously, this is no problem when the work is first commissioned, but if there may be further uses, the client will want to be assured that the artwork is still available when needed.

There are a number of ways of getting over this problem. Perhaps the most satisfactory is for the client to make a good quality scan before returning artwork. This is not expensive, and has great advantages in terms of ease of storage.

G.5 Protecting the Illustrator's ownership

AOI members who wish to protect their ownership rights are strongly advised to use the Ownership of Artwork stickers available from the AOI. These give notice to all those who actually handle the artwork, and help to reinforce trade custom.

Ownership of Artwork stickers should be fixed to the front cover of the artwork or to the artwork itself. Fixing them on the back is ineffective, as they will not be seen.

It is a wise precaution to make the illustrator's ownership of his/her artwork a specific term of the illustrator's standard terms of trade.

Further reading

In place of a formal bibliography, what follows is a selection of books which I can particularly recommend and which might be of interest or use to illustrators. I have not included any legal text books, as these are pretty heavy going.

Publishing Agreements
A Book Of Precedents. ed Charles Clark et al, pub Butterworths.
A bible for those wanting thoroughly to understand their royalty contract, it contains a range of model contracts used in the publishing industry with very helpful notes. Much of the information on royalties in this guide was gleaned from this invaluable reference book.

Between a Rock and a Hard Place
The Problems Facing Freelance Creators in the UK Market Place, Lionel Bently, pub Institute of Employment Rights.
Described as 'A briefing document on behalf of the Creators' Rights Alliance', this small book documents the exploitative practices found in all the creative industries and suggests solutions. Lionel Bently is a Reader in Law at King's College, London. Highly recommended.

Copyright's Highway
**The Law and Lore of Copyright from Gutenberg to the Celestial Jukebox,
Paul Goldstein, pub Hill and Wang (USA)**
Largely USA focussed, a readable general history of copyright which includes
an excellent description of the two competing copyright cultures and an
interesting account of the economic motives behind its history.

Dear Images
**Art, Copyright and Culture. ed Daniel McClean and Karsten Schubert,
pub ICA and Ridinghouse**
Discusses many current copyright issues, including a good account of
Bridgeman v. Corel, which dealt with photographic copyright in two-dimensional
images. Particularly strong on the issues in appropriation art.

Graphic Arts Guild Handbook:
Pricing and Ethical Guidelines. pub Graphic Arts Guild, New York
A useful reference book dealing with current practice in the USA for visual
creators of every kind.

Business and Legal Forms for Illustrators
Tad Crawford, pub Allworth Press, New York
Though intended for the USA market, and though some of the contracts strike
me as a bit over-simplified, this is nevertheless a very useful reference book.

Legal Guide for the Visual Artist
Tad Crawford, pub Madison Square Press, Inc.
USA version of Rights, though it includes a wider range of issues since it
encompasses all the visual arts. Good account of 'Work for Hire'.

Index

Acknowledgements

I have picked the brains of any number of lawyers over the years, but I would particularly like to thank DACS colleagues Anthony Gostyn, Henry Lydiate, Helen Dutta and Camillo Gatta. My special thanks to Mark Stephens and Robert Lands, both from Finers Stephens Innocent. Mark was kind enough to check the first edition of Rights for errors, and Robert has checked this one and has prevented a number of small (and some larger) mistakes from gaining entry, especially in the 'Going to Law' section.

Simon Stern

Credits

The AOI gratefully acknowledge the use of the images created for this publication by the following illustrators:

Kenneth Andsersson www.kennethandersson.com

Paul Bommer www.paulbommer.com

Russell Cobb www.russellcobb.com

Sarah Coleman www.inkymole.com

Adam Graff www.adamgraff.co.uk

Sarah Hanson www.sarahhanson.co.uk

Lyn Moran

Nigel Owen www.nigelowen.com

Harriet Russell www.harrietrussell.co.uk

Andy Smith www.asmithillustration.com

Lasse Skarbövik www.lasseskarbovik.com

Nancy Tolford www.nancytolford.com

Design by Simon Sharville www.simonsharville.co.uk

EMPLOYMENT

FAMILY

CORPORATE

COMMERCIAL
DISPUTE
RESOLUTION

PERSONAL
INJURY

IP MEDIA

PROPERTY

PRIVATE CLIENT

fSi
Finers
Stephens
Innocent

 FSI are proud to be the AOI's solicitors. With over 25 years experience acting for illustrators and visual artists, FSI advise on matters that affect you including copyright issues, contracts and electronic rights.

FSILAW.COM